*The Pastor's Prayerbook*

# *The*
# PASTOR'S PRAYERBOOK

Selected and arranged for various occasions

BY

## *Robert N. Rodenmayer*

Professor of Pastoral Theology
The Church Divinity School of the Pacific

NEW YORK
OXFORD UNIVERSITY PRESS
1960

© 1960 by Oxford University Press, Inc.

Library of Congress Catalogue Card Number: 60-13210

Printed in the United States of America

*To my students*

*past and present*

# Editor's Preface

This book is offered to meet a need of the pastors of all Christian churches, a collection of prayers which follows the rhythm of their days. It will never be possible to collect in one volume all of the prayers which might be used on various occasions but an attempt has been made to provide for all of the minister's main concerns, public and private.

The prayers printed here range from those taken from ancient sources to a number which were written for this book. I have selected them from among something over eighteen thousand prayers, read and noted. Each prayer has been reproduced here using the punctuation and capitalization of pronouns as in the original copy. My thanks are due to many authors, known and unknown, to more than one hundred of my former students at The Church Divinity School of the Pacific, and others, who have made helpful suggestions.

One is limited as well as enriched by his own tradition. Some words which are native to one spiritual household in the Church may need to be changed and adapted to the uses of another. There is no constraint here, only an offering to be used. It is my earnest hope that this collection of prayers may help us to fulfill our ministry.

R. N. R.

*Berkeley, California*
*August,* 1960

# ACKNOWLEDGMENTS

I wish to offer my thanks to a number of authors, holders of copyrights, and publishers, who have permitted me to include prayers in this book. An effort has been made to trace the source of every prayer used, but in some cases this has not been possible. Any errors or omissions on my part are unintentional.

Oxford University Press (New York and London): *Our Bounden Duty*, for prayers by Miles Lowell Yates; *The Kingdom, the Power and the Glory; Daily Prayer*, edited by Dean Eric Milner-White and Canon George W. Briggs, for several prayers by the Editors, and others; *Prayers for the Christian Year* (prepared by the General Assembly of the Church of Scotland); *The Monastic Diurnal*, for one collect; *Let Us Pray; The London Service Book*, for prayers by Canon Briggs, the editor.

Forward Movement Publications (Cincinnati, Ohio): *Prayers New and Old*, edited by Clement W. Welsh; *Prayers for All Occasions*, edited by Francis J. Moore; *Hope and Courage;* and *A Selection of the Prayers of Henry Sylvester Nash*, edited by John W. Suter.

Morehouse-Barlow Co. (New York): *A Book of Prayers*, compiled by John Heuss; *Burial Services*, compiled by Joseph B. Bernardin; *Parent's Prayers*, selected and written by Muriel Streitbert Curtis.

Longmans, Green & Co., Ltd. (London): for permission to reproduce nine prayers from *An Anthology of Prayers*, edited by A. S. T. Fisher; two prayers from *The Priest's Prayer Book*, edited by Littledale & Vaux.

A. R. Mowbray & Co., Ltd. (London): *The Prayer Manual* by Frederick B. Macnutt; *The Conducting of Retreats* by James Wareham; for permission on behalf of Dean E. Milner-White to reprint a prayer from *After the Third Collect*, by Dean Milner-White.

The Student Christian Movement Press Limited (London): *A Book of Prayers for Students; The Abiding*

*Presence* for a prayer by Archbishop William Temple; *A Devotional Diary* by J. H. Oldham; *Prayers of Health and Healing.*

The Pilgrim Press (Boston): *Prayers for the Minister's Day* (1946); *Prayers of the Social Awakening* by Walter Rauschenbusch.

Harper and Brothers (New York): *Prayers for Today,* edited by Samuel McComb.

The Seabury Press (Greenwich, Conn.): Massey H. Shepherd, *Holy Communion: An Anthology of Christian Devotion:* St. Thomas Aquinas, p. 31.

The Protestant Episcopal Diocese of Massachusetts: *Prayers for the Church Service League.*

The Church Pension Fund (New York): *The Book of Offices* (second edition, 1949).

E. P. Dutton & Co., Inc.: for permission to reprint eight prayers from *A Chain of Prayer Across the Ages* compiled by Selina F. Fox.

The British Broadcasting Corporation (London): *New Every Morning* (1936, 1955).

Edinburgh House Press (London): *In His Name,* compiled by George Appleton, published by Edinburgh House Press and Macmillan and Co., for a prayer by Mr. Appleton.

The Church Army in the U. S. A. (New York): for a prayer written for their use.

The Industrial Christian Fellowship (London): for a prayer reprinted in *The Prayer Manual,* edited by Frederick B. Macnutt.

Burns Oates and Washbourne, Ltd. (London): *Praying While You Work,* by Dom Hubert van Zeller.

St. Augustine's College (Canterbury): *Manual of St. Augustine's College.*

Macrae Smith Co. (Philadelphia): *With God in Prayer,* by Charles Henry Brent.

The United Lutheran Church in America (New York): *Occasional Service Book.*

Little, Brown and Co. (Boston): *Prayers Ancient and Modern,* selected by Mary Wilder Tileston, for a prayer by William Angus Knight.

The Dell Publishing Co., Inc. (New York): *Book of Prayers,* edited by Leon and Elfrieda McCauley.

John Wallace Suter, *Prayers of the Spirit.*

Stephen Fielding Bayne, Jr., S.T.D., Executive Officer of the Anglican Communion, *Prayers for the Diocese of Olympia,* for a prayer of his authorship.

Professor Reinhold Niebuhr for two prayers of his authorship.

Professor Gregory Vlastos for a prayer of his which was first printed in *The Church Review,* Vol. XV, No. 4, May 1956.

Robert Arthur Miller for a prayer from *In Weakness Strength,* published by The Protestant Episcopal Diocese of Mass.

Douglas H. Crick, retired Bishop of Chester, for a prayer of his printed in *The Prayer Manual,* edited by Frederick B. Macnutt.

William Appleton Lawrence, retired Bishop of Western Massachusetts, for a number of prayers from *Prayers for Our Ministry,* compiled by Thomas Frederick Davies, Bishop of Western Massachusetts (1911-36).

Eric Symes Abbott, Dean of Westminster, for permission to use a prayer from the Office of the Royal Maundy.

W. R. Matthews, Dean of St. Paul's, for permission to reprint a prayer from the Use of St. Paul's Cathedral.

Barton, Mayhew and Co. (London) for a prayer by Miss
L. H. M. Soulsby, *An Anthology of Prayers*, edited by
A. S. T. Fisher.

Lady Sykes for permission to use prayers by Percy
Dearmer.

The Superior General, the Society of St. John the Evangelist, for permission to use two prayers by Richard
Meux Benson.

Leslie S. Hunter, Bishop of Sheffield, for a prayer of his
printed in *New Every Morning*.

My thanks are extended to Dean Sherman E. Johnson
for permission to use a number of prayers written by
him over a period of years and not previously published,
also to several others who have allowed me to use their
unpublished prayers or who have written prayers especially for this book: Edward Lambe Parsons, retired
Bishop of California; William Fisher Lewis, Bishop of
Nevada; Charles Francis Hall, Bishop of New Hampshire; Canon Theodore O. Wedel of the Washington
Cathedral; Professor Charles F. Whiston; Chaplain Robert Plumb; the Rev. Charles S. Martin; the Rev. Max L.
Drake; the Rev. Derwent A. Suthers; Richard Feller;
Helen Beck; Carol Christopher Drake.

Finally, I wish to acknowledge a personal debt of gratitude to the Rev. Dr. John W. Suter for much valuable
assistance generously given; to my colleagues the Rev.
Drs. James Bennett Pritchard for the idea of the book
and for helpful criticism, and Massey Hamilton Shepherd, Jr., for help in tracing sources; to Canon Wedel
for the hospitality of the College of Preachers in Washington, where the major part of the research for this
book was done in the winter of 1959; to Marie Petersen
for typing and correcting the entire manuscript; to my
wife for many hours of editorial assistance, encouragement, and support.

                                                    R. N. R.

# CONTENTS

*The Pastor's Prayerbook*

# I

## MORNING

### –1– *In the Morning*

O God, the King eternal, who dividest the day from the darkness, and turnest the shadow of death into the morning; Drive far off from us all wrong desires, incline our hearts to keep thy law, and guide our feet into the way of peace; that having done thy will with cheerfulness while it was day, we may, when the night cometh, rejoice to give thee thanks; through Jesus Christ our Lord.

### –2– *This Day*

Fix thou our steps, O Lord, that we stagger not at the uneven motions of the world, but go steadily on our way, neither censuring our journey by the weather we meet, nor turning aside for anything that may befall us; through Jesus Christ our Lord.

### –3– *A Morning Dedication*

And since it is of thy mercy, O gracious Father, that another day is added to our lives; We here dedicate both our souls and our bodies to thee

3

and thy service, in a sober, righteous, and godly
life: in which resolution, do thou, O merciful
God confirm and strengthen us; that, as we grow
in age, we may grow in grace, and in the knowledge of our Lord and Saviour Jesus Christ.

## –4– *The Daily Walk*

O God, who orderest the common things of the
common day, dignify by thy presence and aid
the trivial round and routine tasks of thy servant
whose hope is in thee, that least duties may be
grandly done and all activities marked with the
seal of thy righteousness; through Jesus Christ
our Lord.

## –5– *Praise and Prayer*

O Lord our God, Who hast chased the slumber
from our eyes, and once more assembled us to
lift up our hands unto Thee and to praise Thy
just judgments, accept our prayers and supplications, and give us faith and love. Bless our
coming in and our going out, our thoughts,
words, and works, and let us begin this day with
the praise of the unspeakable sweetness of Thy
mercy. Hallowed be Thy name. Thy kingdom
come; through Jesus Christ our Lord.

*–6– Morning Litany*

O God, the Father of Heaven,
  O God, the Son, Redeemer of the world,
  O God, the Holy Ghost, Sanctifier of Thy
      people:
    Hear us, we beseech Thee, O Lord.

We, in communion with all Thy saints in all ages, with patriarchs and prophets, with apostles and martyrs, with all who have passed from us into Thy Presence,

We, who are still striving to do and to bear Thy blessed will on earth,

Adore Thee, and offer to Thee our praises, thanksgivings and supplications.
    Hear us, we beseech Thee, O Lord.

We pray Thee to reveal to us
  The gladness of Thy service,
  The beauty of Thy perfect will,
  The power of Thy presence in our hearts.
  Hear us, we beseech Thee, O Lord.

Help us to forgive as we would be forgiven, dwelling neither in speech nor thought upon offences committed against us, but loving one another as Thou lovest us.
    Hear us, we beseech Thee, O Lord.

Make us of quick and tender conscience, that we may follow every suggestion of Thine indwelling Spirit.
    Hear us, we beseech Thee, O Lord.

May no perplexity create in us an impatient spirit, no temptation lead us into sin, no sorrow hide Thy loving will from us.

Hear us, we beseech Thee, O Lord.

Gracious Father, Who willest us to cast all our care on Thee Who carest for us, preserve us from faithless fears and selfish anxieties, and grant that no clouds of this mortal life may hide from us the light of the love which is immortal and which Thou hast manifested to us in Jesus Christ our Lord, but that we may this day walk in the Light of Thy countenance, be guided by Thine eye, sanctified by Thy Spirit, and be enabled to live to Thy glory.

Hear us, we beseech Thee, O Lord.

## –7– *A Pure Intention*

Almighty God, who alone gavest us the breath of life, and alone canst keep alive in us the holy desires thou dost impart; We beseech thee, for thy compassion's sake, to sanctify all our thoughts and endeavours; that we may neither begin an action without a pure intention nor continue it without thy blessing. And grant that, having the eyes of the mind opened to behold things invisible and unseen, we may in heart be inspired by thy wisdom, and in work be upheld by thy strength, and in the end be accepted of thee as thy faithful servants; through Jesus Christ our Saviour.

### –8– *For Simplicity*

O Saviour, who in the completeness of Thy manhood art still Babe of Bethlehem and Child of Nazareth, restore in me the simplicity I have tampered with, the transparency I have obscured, the childlikeness I have lost, that the shattered fragments of my innocence may be assembled anew in the beauty of Thy sanctity; who with the Father and the Holy Ghost art God forever and ever.

### –9– *For Cheerfulness*

O God, renew our spirits by thy Holy Spirit, and draw our hearts this morning unto thyself, that our work may not be a burden, but a delight; and give us such a mighty love to thee as may sweeten all our obedience. Let us not serve with the spirit of bondage as slaves, but with cheerfulness and gladness, as children, delighting ourselves in thee and rejoicing in thy wishes for the sake of Jesus Christ.

### –10– *For Guidance*

O God, by whom the meek are guided in judgment, and light riseth up in darkness for the godly; Grant us, in all our doubts and uncertainties, the grace to ask what thou wouldest have us to do, that the Spirit of Wisdom may

save us from all false choices, and that in thy
light we may see light, and in thy straight path
may not stumble; through Jesus Christ our Lord.

*–11– For God's Will*

Lord, make me conscious of Thy holiness and
majesty: teach me to know and do Thy will:
pour into my heart such love towards Thee, that,
loving Thee above all things, I may obtain Thy
gracious promises; through Jesus Christ our Lord.

*–12– For Today*

O God, give me strength to live another day. Let
me not turn coward before its difficulties or
prove recreant to its duties. Let me not lose faith
in my fellow men. Keep me sweet and sound of
heart, in spite of ingratitude, treachery, or mean-
ness. Preserve me from minding little stings or
giving them. Help me to keep my heart clean,
and to live so honestly and fearlessly that no
outward failure can dishearten me or take away
the joy of conscious integrity. Open wide the
eyes of my soul that I may see good in all things.
Grant me this day some new vision of thy truth,
inspire me with the spirit of joy and gladness,
and make me the cup of strength to suffering
souls; in the name of the strong Deliverer, our
only Lord and Saviour, Jesus Christ.

*–13– For the Joy of Our Lord*

Help us this day, O God, to serve thee devoutly,
and the world busily. May we do our work
wisely, give succour secretly, go to our meat
appetitely, sit thereat discreetly, arise temper-
ately, please our friend duly, go to our bed mer-
rily, and sleep surely; for the joy of our Lord,
Jesus Christ.

# II

## Noon

### *–14– At Noon*

Blessed Saviour, who at this hour didst hang upon the cross stretching forth thy loving arms, grant that all mankind may look unto thee and be saved.

Almighty Saviour, who at mid-day didst call thy servant St. Paul to be an apostle to the Gentiles; we beseech thee to illumine the world with the radiance of thy glory, that all nations may come and worship thee, who art with the Father and the Holy Ghost, one God, world without end.

Give peace for all time, O Lord, and fill my heart and the hearts of all men everywhere with the spirit of our Lord Jesus Christ.

### *–15– A Noontime Prayer*

Lord Jesus, who didst stretch out thine arms of love on the hard wood of the Cross, that all men might come within the reach of thy saving embrace, clothe us in thy spirit, that we, stretching forth our hands in loving labor for others, may

bring those who know thee not to the knowledge
and love of thee, who with the Father and the
Holy Ghost livest and reignest one God.

## −16− *For Missions*

O God, who hast made of one blood all nations
of men for to dwell on the face of the whole
earth, and didst send thy blessed Son to preach
peace to them that are far off and to them that
are nigh; Grant that all men everywhere may
seek after thee and find thee. Bring the nations
into thy fold, pour out thy Spirit upon all flesh,
and hasten thy kingdom; through the same thy
Son Jesus Christ our Lord.

## −17− *For Workers in Lonely Places*

O Father Almighty and God of all comfort;
Look with compassion, we beseech thee, upon
the little companies of our faithful brethren
who, in lonely places of the world, are striving
to uphold the banner of the Cross. If the comfort
of human sympathy seem far from them, be thou
their close companion, and pour into their hearts
the spirit of hope; that they may steadfastly persevere, and be of good courage because of thy
word, knowing that their labor is not in vain;
through Jesus Christ our Lord.

### –18– *For Missionaries*

O Thou who dost call men and women to carry
the good news of Jesus Christ to all nations;
Grant thy strengthening grace to all who have
responded to thy call. Give them vision to see
the greatness of their service, and humility to see
their own unworthiness. Guide them in all their
preparation, enriching the good gifts which they
already possess, and supplying those which they
lack. Give them happiness and peace, insight and
adaptability, courage and good judgment. Make
them ready to learn as well as to give, that they
may truly show forth Jesus, not only in their
words but in their lives.

### –19– *For All Saints*

O Almighty God, who hast knit together thine
elect in one communion and fellowship, in the
mystical body of thy Son Christ our Lord; Grant
us grace so to follow thy blessed Saints in all
virtuous and godly living, that we may come to
those unspeakable joys which thou hast prepared
for those who unfeignedly love thee; through
the same thy Son Jesus Christ our Lord.

### –20– *For Faith*

Almighty and everlasting **God**, who **dost en-**
kindle the flame of thy love in the hearts of the

Saints; Grant to us, thy humble servants, the same faith and power of love; that, as we rejoice in their triumphs, we may profit by their examples; through Jesus Christ our Lord.

# III

## NIGHT

### –21– A Collect for Aid Against Perils

Lighten our darkness, we beseech thee, O Lord;
and by thy great mercy defend us from all perils
and dangers of this night; for the love of thy
only Son, our Saviour, Jesus Christ.

### –22– An Evening Offering

O Thou unchanging lover of men, who dost continually make new the failures and imperfections
of men, accept, we beseech Thee, the offering
of what we have done, and left undone, and
done amiss this day. Meet our imperfection with
Thy perfection, our weakness with Thy life, our
sins with Thy transforming love, and accept and
make perfect; through these our imperfect
prayers.

### –23– In the Silent Hours

Be present, O merciful God, and protect us
through the silent hours of this night, so that we
who are fatigued by the changes and chances
of this fleeting world, may repose upon thy eter-

nal changelessness; through Jesus Christ our Lord.

## –24– *For Common Blessings*

Father of lights, from whose unshadowed home above comes every good and perfect gift, I receive as from Thy hand my share in the common blessings which, without respect of persons, hourly descend upon mankind. I thank Thee for the special tokens of Thy friendship and personal care that have made me glad this day. Help me to use these and all Thy bounties according to Thy design, that my whole life may be a hymn of praise to Thee; through Jesus Christ our Lord.

## –25– *For Blessings of the Day*

O God, who art the life of mortal men, the light of the faithful, the strength of those who labour, and the repose of the dead; We thank thee for the timely blessings of the day, and humbly supplicate thy merciful protection all this night. Bring us, we beseech thee, in safety to the morning hours; through him who died for us and rose again, thy Son, our Saviour Jesus Christ.

## –26– *Peace and Safety*

I will lay me down in peace and take my rest: for thou, Lord, only, makest us to dwell in safety.

Thou, O Christ, art in the midst of us and we are called by thy Name; leave us not, O Lord our God.

Save us, O Lord, while waking, guard us while sleeping; that awake we may watch with Christ, and asleep we may rest in peace.

### *–27– The Veil of Night*

O God, who hast drawn over weary day the restful veil of night, wrap our consciences in heavenly peace. Lift from our hands our tasks, and all through the night bear in Thy bosom the full weight of our burdens and sorrows, that in untroubled slumber we may press our weakness close to Thy strength, and win new power for the morrow's duty from Thee who givest Thy beloved sleep.

### *–28– At Night*

O Lord, support us all the day long, until the shadows lengthen and the evening comes, and the busy world is hushed, and the fever of life is over, and our work is done. Then in thy mercy grant us a safe lodging, and a holy rest, and peace at the last.

### -29- A Commendation

God be in my head,
And in my understanding;
God be in my eyes,
And in my looking;
God be in my mouth,
And in my speaking;
God be in my heart,
And in my thinking;
God be at mine end,
And at my departing.

# IV

## The Ministry

### -30- For Those Called to the Ministry

Almighty God, the giver of all good gifts, who of thy divine providence hast appointed divers Orders in thy Church; Give thy grace, we humbly beseech thee, to all those who are to be called to any office and administration in the same; and so replenish them with the truth of thy doctrine, and endue them with innocency of life, that they may faithfully serve before thee, to the glory of thy great Name, and the benefit of thy holy Church; through Jesus Christ our Lord.

### -31- For Worthiness

Remember, O Lord, what thou hast wrought in us, and not what we deserve; and, as thou hast called us to thy service, make us worthy of our calling; through Jesus Christ our Lord.

### -32- For Gladness

O God, author of the world's joy, bearer of the world's pain; Make us glad we are men, and that we have inherited the world's burden; de-

liver us from the luxury of cheap melancholy; and, at the heart of all our trouble and sorrow, let unconquerable gladness dwell.

## –33– *The Quickening Spirit*

All through this day, O Lord, let me touch as many lives as possible for Thee; and every life I touch, do Thou, by Thy Holy Spirit, quicken, whether through the word I speak, the prayer I breathe, the letters I write, or the life I live; in the name of Jesus Christ.

## –34– *For Our Ministry*

Remember all those who do the Lord's work in the ministry and conduct of souls. Give us, we beseech Thee, O Father, great gifts and great holiness, that wisely and charitably, diligently and zealously, prudently and acceptably, we may be guides to the blind, comforters to the sad and weary; that we may strengthen the weak and confirm the strong, boldly rebuke sin, patiently suffer for the truth, and be exemplary in our lives; that in all our actions and sermons, in our discipline and ministrations, we may advance the good of souls, and the honour of our Lord Jesus Christ; grant this for the sake of Thy Son our Lord.

#### –35– *For My People*

Almighty God, look mercifully, I beseech Thee, on all my spiritual children; grant them to grow in grace and the knowledge of Thee, guide them in all doubt, comfort them in all trouble, strengthen them in all weakness, and vouchsafe that my ministrations may be profitable to their souls; through Jesus Christ our Lord.

#### –36– *In Controversy*

O Lord and Saviour Christ, Who camest not to strive nor cry, give unto me, in whatsoever contention I may be, a wise, a sober, a patient, an understanding, a peaceable, a courageous heart. Grant me always to speak Thy truth in love, and so to present it that it may be loved; for Thy mercies' sake.

#### –37– *For Charity*

O Lord, grant me so to love thee, with all my heart, with all my mind, and with all my soul, and my neighbor for thy sake, that the grace of charity and brotherly love may dwell in me, and all envy, harshness, and ill-will may die in me; and fill my heart with feelings of love, kindness, and compassion so that, by constantly rejoicing in the happiness and good success of others, by sympathizing with them in their sorrows and

putting away all harsh judgments and envious thoughts, I may follow thee, who art thyself the true and perfect love, Jesus Christ our Lord.

## −38− For Steadiness

O God who has made us in thine image, and who sustains us in our failures, preserve us, we beseech thee, from presumption and despair, and grant that we may serve thee with steadiness and patience; through Jesus Christ our Lord.

## −39− For the Ministry

O God, we beseech thee, grant thy grace to all whom thou hast called to the ministry of thy Church, that they may diligently teach thy people from the Scriptures and administer the sacraments in accordance with thy will; that they may banish and drive away from the Church all erroneous doctrines contrary to thy Word; that they may be diligent in prayer and in reading the Scriptures, and in such studies as help to the knowledge of the same, laying aside the study of the world and the flesh; that they may frame and fashion themselves, and their families, according to the doctrine of Christ, and so make them wholesome examples and patterns to the flock of Christ; and finally that they may maintain and forward quietness, peace, and love among all Christian people; to the end that the good work which thou hast begun in them may

be accomplished; through the same thy Son Jesus
Christ our Lord.

### -40- *Power and Might*

Let us pray that we may be so made new that
God may send us to do his work. Peace be unto
you: As the Father hath sent me, even so send
I you.

Lord of all power and might, fill our lives with
the joy of thy Word and the courage of thine
apostles, that having caught the vision of thy
Kingdom we may proclaim it with power and a
glad heart, to the salvation of men's souls and
the creation of a better order more conformed
to the pattern of thy Kingdom; through Jesus
Christ our Lord.

### -41- *For Our Bishop*

Almighty and everlasting God, have mercy upon
thy servant, (N.), our Bishop, and after thy
great goodness, direct him in the way of eternal
salvation: that by thy grace he may desire those
things that are well-pleasing unto thee, and with
all his might perform the same, through Jesus
Christ our Lord.

### -42- *For Bishops, Clergy and Ministers*

O Lord God Almighty, who didst endue thine apostles so richly with the gifts of the Holy Spirit, grant to all thy servants who minister and teach in thy holy name, the spirit of wisdom and love, that in all their words and deeds they may seek thy glory and the increase of thy kingdom; through Jesus Christ our Lord.

### -43- *For Colleagues in the Ministry*

Abide now in strength, O God, with those who serve with me the congregations of this community. Like Thy Church in all the years, let us now be the body of Thy Christ—his hands our hands, his tongue our tongue, his feet our feet. In Thy name let us speak Thy word, and in Thy power lift up the weary and comfort the sorrowing. Grant that no jealousy of each other may silence Thy Kingdom's praise, and empower us all to be in Thee the prophets of Thy purpose and the priests of Thy grace. Through Jesus Christ our Lord.

### -44- *Change of Circumstances*

Almighty God, heavenly Father, who hast graciously prolonged my life to this time, and by the change of outward things which I am now to make, callest me to a change of inward af-

fections, and to a reformation of my thoughts, words and practices; vouchsafe, merciful Lord, that this call may not be in vain. Forgive me whatever has been amiss in the state which I am now leaving, idleness and neglect of thy word and worship. Grant me the grace of thy Holy Spirit, that the course which I am now beginning may proceed according to thy laws, and end in the enjoyment of thy favour. Give me, O Lord, pardon and peace, that I may serve thee with humble confidence, and after this life enjoy thy presence eternally, for Jesus Christ's sake.

## –45– *New Truth*

O God, whose revelation never faileth and who showest a new aspect of thy eternal truth to each generation, grant unto us to see the truth as thou dost set it before us in this our day and to strive for its realization among our fellow men; through Jesus Christ our Lord.

## –46– *For the Increase of the Ministry*

O Almighty God, look mercifully upon the world which thou hast redeemed by the blood of thy dear Son, and incline the hearts of many to dedicate themselves to the sacred Ministry of thy Church; through the same thy Son Jesus Christ our Lord.

# V

## MEETINGS (CHURCH)

### –47– *For the Parish Family*

O God, in whom all the families of the earth are
blessed, visit with thy loving-kindness the homes
in which our people dwell; give them tenderness and patience, forbearance and love, that together we may be one body in thy Son, our
Saviour Jesus Christ.

### –48– *For a Meeting*

O God, who did preside at the council of the
blessed apostles, guide our deliberations, we beseech thee, and direct our motives, that our
thoughts, words, and actions in this meeting may
be according to thy holy will; through Jesus
Christ our Lord.

### –49– *For Parish Organizations*

O Lord, whose holy apostle has taught us that
as members of thy body we all have our part to
play in the whole life of thy Church, we thank
thee for this work which thou hast given us to
do together; and we pray thee to give us grace

25

to persevere in it, and through it to serve thee
to thy honor and glory.

### *–50– For a Committee*

Bless, we beseech thee, O God, the work of this
committee; grant to its members clarity of
thought, evenness of temper, and willingness to
persevere in thy service; through Jesus Christ
our Lord.

### *–51– For Our Work*

O God, with whom a thousand years are as one
day, and who hast called us whose lives pass as
a watch in the night unto thy service; Grant
that we may so do our work that it shall not
need to be undone. Stay, we beseech thee, the
fever in our hearts, and help us to walk in the
light of thine own eternity, through Jesus Christ
our Lord.

### *–52– For an Annual Parish Meeting*

Grant, O Lord, that thy Holy Spirit may preside over us now in all our concerns and deliberations for the welfare of this parish. We thank
thee for all the blessings of the past year, and
pray that we may go together from strength to
strength in the year before us. Help us all to
dedicate ourselves to thee, and to be ready to

make sacrifice of time and money for the extension of thy kingdom.

Guide us, we beseech thee, in the choice of our Wardens, Vestrymen, and Delegates to Convention, and may they discharge their duties faithfully.

We praise thee for those thy servants who labored and worshipped here before us, and especially for those who have departed this life since we last met together. Grant to them eternal rest, O Lord, and let thy light perpetual shine upon them; through Jesus Christ our Lord.

### –53– *For the Altar Guild*

O Loving Saviour, we pray thee to send thy blessing upon this Altar Guild and the work of all its members; give us thy grace that we may be loyal to thy Holy Church, and faithful in our care of holy things. Grant that as we adorn and make ready thy Altar we may learn greater love and reverence for all that belongs to thy service, and through all outward symbols come to a clearer vision of the inward and spiritual truth taught by them. We ask this for thy sake, O Blessed Lord and Master.

### -54- *For Parish Leaders*

Vouchsafe, O Lord, to thy servants to whom the
affairs of this Parish are committed, prudence,
justice and charity, that they may be of one
mind and one heart in the upbuilding of the
Church, and in the spread of thy kingdom;
through Jesus Christ our Lord.

### -55- *A Church Governing Body*

O God, who has given into our hands the ministry of reconciliation, help us to fulfill our responsibilities in thy Name with wisdom, cheerfulness
and honesty; through Jesus Christ our Lord.

### -56- *A Vestry Meeting*

Almighty God, giver of all gifts, grant to the
members of this Vestry, wisdom to avoid false
choices, courage to follow our Lord's teachings,
vision to see thy true calling for this parish, and
the grace humbly to acknowledge thy Church
universal, through Jesus Christ our Lord.

### -57- *For a Vestry*

Blessed Lord, who hast called us to this office
in thy Church, guide us, we beseech thee, in our
deliberations, so that all our aims and purposes
may be to the strengthening of the work in this

parish and the support of the Church's mission throughout the world; through Jesus Christ our Lord.

### –58– *For the Women's Division*

O Lord, without whom our labor is but lost, and with whom Thy little ones go forth as the mighty; we humbly beseech Thee to prosper all works in Thy Church undertaken according to Thy holy will, especially the work of the Women's Division, and grant to Thy laborers a pure intention, patient faith, sufficient success upon earth, and the blessedness of serving Thee in heaven; through Jesus Christ our Lord.

### –59– *For a Women's Guild*

O God, who has called us to serve thee with gladness, bless, we beseech thee, the purposes of this group assembled in thy Name; give them charity with one another, generosity in their good works, and devotion to the spread of thy kingdom.

### –60– *A Men's Guild*

O God, who has given each of us a man's job to do in thy world, grant that in our being and in our doing we may faithfully and cheerfully do thy will; through Jesus Christ our Lord.

## –61– *For Servers and Acolytes*

Almighty and everlasting God, who givest grace to those who minister; bestow Thy blessing, we pray Thee, upon Thy servants appointed to serve those who stand before Thine Altar. Give them such seriousness of life, that the services in which they engage may be to their profit and spiritual good. Through their association with holy places and things may they grow in the Christian life, and by their service in the house where Thou dost manifest Thine honor and glory, may they be prepared for that House not made with hands, eternal in the heavens; through Jesus Christ our Lord.

## –62– *Young People*

O God, who hast made us in thy image, we give thee thanks for friends and homes, for youth and strength, for hopes and dreams; help us to be honest, to live up to the best we know, and to grow in the knowledge and love of thy Son our Saviour Jesus Christ.

## –63– *Youth Sunday*

O God, who dost behold and bless the young men and women in thy household the Church, look with thy favor upon the young people gathered here in thy Name and presence; guide

their growing minds and bodies, kindle their
imagination with high resolves, lead their eager
independence into good channels and knit them
close to thee and to their Christian brothers and
sisters in every land; through him who came
to set men free, thy Son, Jesus Christ our Lord.

## –64– *Extension of the Kingdom*

Almighty God, our Heavenly Father, bless, we
pray thee, our work for the extension of thy
kingdom, and make us so thankful for the precious gift to us of thy beloved Son, that we may
pray fervently, labor diligently, and give liberally
to make him known to all nations as their Saviour
and their King; through the same Jesus Christ
our Lord.

# VI

## Meetings (Community)

### -65- *An Invocation*

Be with us, O God, in all our enterprises; purify our intentions, strengthen our purposes, and grant that in serving our fellowmen we may serve thee; through Jesus Christ our Lord.

### -66- *For a Business or Service Club*

Almighty God, whose great commandment is that we shall love our neighbors as ourselves, and who hast taught us that we should do to others as we would have them do to us, we ask thy blessing upon the work of this Club. As our purpose is to help our fellowmen and to promote all that is good in the life of our community, so we pray that thou wilt strengthen our hands in all our undertakings, and that our work may spread the spirit of fellowship and goodwill among all men.

### -67- *For Social Service*

O Lord, our heavenly Father, whose blessed Son came not to be ministered unto, but to minister; we beseech Thee to bless all those who labor in

social service work. Endue them with wisdom,
patience, and courage to strengthen the weak, to
raise up those who fall, and to comfort the suffering, the friendless, and the needy; that, being
inspired by Thy love, they may worthily minister in Thy name, for the sake of Him who laid
down His life for us, the same Thy Son our
Saviour Jesus Christ.

## –68– *For Social Agencies*

Almighty God, whose compassions fail not, and
who hast taught us to have compassion upon
those in need, prosper, we pray thee the work
of our social agencies, and especially ——— Stir
up the wills of all our people to support them
in the relief of want and suffering, and let us
not rest until we have provided for the needs
of thy children, giving generously as thou hast
given to us.

## –69– *For Alcoholics*

O God, our Father, who knowest all thy children, deal graciously with us in our needs; give
strength to the weak, courage to the half-hearted,
freedom to those who have been enslaved. Help
us, who are helpless without thee, to help each
other in thy name.

### –70– *God's Family*

Bind, O God, the heart of every man to his neighbor, and the hearts of all men to thee, in whom the whole family in heaven and earth are one; through the power of the Holy Ghost.

# VII

## CIVIL AND PATRIOTIC

-71- *A Civic Election*

Guide, O Lord, we pray Thee, the mayor and
corporation with all, from the greatest to the
least, who share in the ordering of this town (*or*
city), and give strength, honour, and charity to
us and to our fellow citizens; that we may exercise our votes as in Thy sight, and seeking not
our own, may see ever before us the vision of
that free city, perfect in the heavens, whose
builder and maker is God; through Jesus Christ
our Lord.

-72- *During an Election*

Almighty God, the fountain of all wisdom, guide
and direct, we humbly beseech thee, the minds
of all those who are called at this time to exercise
the responsible duty of electing fit persons to
serve in the government of this nation (*or* of this
state *or* city *or* town). Grant that the effect and
right issue of their choice may promote thy glory
and the welfare of this people; and to all those
who shall be elected, give, we pray thee, the
spirit of wisdom, courage, sympathy, and true
godliness. And this we ask for the sake of our
Lord and Saviour, Jesus Christ.

*–73– Before an Election*

Almighty God, who dost hold us to account for
the use of all our powers and privileges; guide,
we pray thee, the people of these United States
in the election of their rulers and representatives;
that by wise legislation and faithful administration the rights of all may be protected, and our
nation enabled to fulfill thy purposes; through
Jesus Christ our Lord.

*–74– For Local Government*

Grant, O God, that Christian people may come
to undertake the work of local government as a
vocation and ministry; that they may bring to
their work brains that think, and hearts that feel;
that they may have ideals, imagination, wisdom
and courage; that they may never be enslaved by
routine and convention and popular opinion, but
ever be upheld by thy free spirit, through the
grace of our Lord Jesus Christ.

*–75– For Civic Officials and Servants*

We pray, O Lord, for all those in our community who are responsible for our civic welfare,
health and security. May thy Holy Spirit guide
our Councilors that they may have a care only
for what will promote good government; and to
all others in positions of responsibility give such

a sense of duty that no self-interest shall turn them from it. We also remember before thee those who are employed in our service in dangerous or lowly work; for we are all members one of another and all our labor is honorable in thy sight. Help us, each one, to do well the work we have to do, for the good of all.

### –76– *For Those in Authority*

O Lord God Almighty, guide, we pray thee, all those to whom thou hast committed the government of this nation, and grant to them at this time special gifts of wisdom and understanding, of counsel and strength; that upholding what is right, and following what is true, they may obey thy holy will and fulfill thy divine purpose; through Jesus Christ our Lord.

### –77– *For Our Country*

Almighty God, who hast given us this good land for our heritage; We humbly beseech thee that we may always prove ourselves a people mindful of thy favour and glad to do thy will. Bless our land with honourable industry, sound learning, and pure manners. Save us from violence, discord, and confusion; from pride and arrogancy, and from every evil way. Defend our liberties, and fashion into one united people the multitudes brought hither out of many kindreds and tongues. Endue with the spirit of wisdom

those to whom in thy Name we entrust the authority of government, that there may be justice and peace at home, and that, through obedience to thy law, we may show forth thy praise among the nations of the earth. In the time of prosperity, fill our hearts with thankfulness, and in the day of trouble, suffer not our trust in thee to fail; all which we ask through Jesus Christ our Lord.

### –78– *For Our Nation*

Almighty God, Ruler of all the peoples of the earth: Forgive, we beseech thee, our shortcomings as a nation; purify our hearts to see and love the truth; give wisdom to our counselors and steadfastness to our people; and bring us at last to that fair city of peace whose foundations are mercy, justice and good-will, whose Builder and Maker thou art; through thy Son, Jesus Christ our Lord.

### –79– *For Those in the Armed Forces*

O Lord God of hosts, stretch forth, we pray thee, thine almighty arm to strengthen the men and women of our armed forces. Keep them temperate in all things, that they may serve thee without stumbling and without stain. For their homes, give them steadfast loyalty through all the days of separation; for their church, give them reverence and devotion; and grant that, re-

turning with greater insight into thy purpose, they may lead us into greater service in thy kingdom; through Jesus Christ our Lord.

## –80– *For Chaplains in the Armed Forces*

Blessed Lord, who didst commission thy disciples to continue the work which the Father sent thee into the world to do, support, we beseech thee, with thy Holy Spirit, those who minister in the Armed Forces of our country. Give them grace to preach thy Gospel both by word and deed; strengthen them in their temptation and make them courageous in the perils of their calling that they may glorify thee before all men: and do thou hold them ever in thy gracious keeping.

## –81– *Commissioning a Ship*

Almighty God, Who hast given us this good land for our heritage; we humbly beseech Thee that we may always prove ourselves a people mindful of Thy favor and glad to do Thy will. Bless this ship which is here commissioned to serve in the Navy of the United States. Grant that in the performance of her duties she may be found worthy of our trust and of the flag unfurled from her mast, that in her fearlessly going forth she may hasten the freedom and peace of the oppressed peoples of the earth and in her returning be a haven of refuge to the sick and the weary.

Accept our prayers for those who in this ship shall commit their lives to the perils of the deep. Support them in the day of battle and keep them safe from all evil. Endue them with courage and loyalty and grant that in all things they may serve without reproach. All of which we ask in thy name.

*–82– For a Graduation Review*

O God, our Heavenly Father, bless we beseech thee these young men (and women) who at this time are to be presented in Graduation Review. Protect and assist them as they serve their country at home and abroad; by land, by sea or by air.

Strengthen them that they may overcome temptation and make them courageous in the perils of their calling. Grant that in distant lands they may so frame and fashion themselves according to thy commandments that they become wholesome examples to the flock of Christ and credits to this Nation.

Make them to know that the service they are giving is of the greatest importance to the security and peace of all mankind; that thy kingdom may be advanced in the earth through Jesus Christ our Lord.

*–83– For Sound Government in the Nation*

Almighty God, our Heavenly Father, bless our country that it may be a blessing to the world; grant that our ideals and aspirations may be in accordance with thy will, and help us to see ourselves as others see us. Keep us from hypocrisy in feeling or action. Grant us sound government and just laws, good education and a clean press, simplicity and justice in our relations with one another, and, above all, a spirit of service which will abolish pride of place and inequality of opportunity; through Jesus Christ our Lord.

*–84– National Responsibility*

O God, who hast called our nation to a place of trust and responsibility throughout the world, we humbly thank thee for all the ways in which thou hast blessed and guided us unto this day. We confess before thee with shame all that has been evil in our history, and all that even now makes us unworthy to be called a Christian nation. Take from us we pray thee, all pride and greed and injustice, and grant to us the spirit of unselfish service which alone can make us great; and may the love of Christ be so truly shown forth among us, that his Name may be glorified among all nations; through the same Jesus Christ our Lord.

# VIII

## Occasions

### –85– *For a School*

O God, who art Lord of time and dost stand
at the gate of the years, we ask thy blessing
upon this school (————), its students, faculty,
alumni, trustees, employees and benefactors, and
all who love and help it. Make it over according to thy will; watch our goings out and our
comings in; overrule our decisions; preserve us
from sloth, discouragement and pride, and fit us
to do thy work with joy and eagerness. In thy
good time grant us that success which is according to thy will; through Jesus Christ our Lord.

### –86– *For a Commencement*

Almighty God, maker and sustainer of all that
is, who hast created us thy children and dost
set us straight when our ways have gone crooked,
we offer thee thanks and praise. Thou hast given
us searching minds that we may trace the course
of life and seek out the causes of events. Thou
hast made us to plant and reap, to compose music
in harmony, and to fashion buildings and pic-
tures in line and form. By thy help we remember the past and preserve its record for the gen-

erations yet to come. Justice and right dealing are thy gifts. Through thy prophets and wise men thou hast taught us to hate falsehood and hast exposed the wily arguments of those who would conceal what is true. Thou hast made us eager to know all that the mind of man can discover and hast given us such courage and industry as we possess. We bless thee for having led our fathers to this fair land and for inspiring them to found a university here. Keep us alert in spirit and loyal to thy truth which has been discovered; preserve us from faithless impatience, from pride, sloth and cheapness, and from doing any shoddy or unworthy work. As thou hast made us free, so preserve our liberties and silence the fearful voices of any who would hold us back from knowing and doing the truth. Where we go astray, correct us; where we are ignorant, let those who follow supply our lack; where we are corrupted through prejudice, pride or self-seeking, make us better men. And, since we are restless until we find ourselves at rest as thy children, bring us, by way of the knowledge of thy world, back to thee; that this university and this nation may know thee as the author of all truth and may do thy will, and that thy people may find peace and blessing; all which we ask for Jesus Christ's sake.

## –87– *For Commencements*

O God who knowest our needs and our desires, bless, we pray thee, our new beginnings. Watch over those who wonder and learn and grow in understanding; purify our motives and purposes and give us a measure of usefulness in the world which thou hast made and redeemed through Jesus Christ our Lord.

## –88– *At a Graduation*

O God, we ask thy blessing upon this school (college): its teachers, students, administrators and benefactors; prosper its life in this community, and grant to its graduates a readiness to support the right as they see the right, and the satisfaction of usefulness in the world which thou hast made; through Jesus Christ our Lord.

## –89– *A Nurses' Graduation*

O God, giver of life and health, who came among us as one who serves, behold and bless these young women who are assuming responsibility as custodians of the crises of life; give them wisdom and skill, patience and cheerfulness, a light step and a steady hand in thy service, through Jesus Christ our Lord.

*-90- For One Awaiting Trial*

O God, whose property is always to have mercy when we are hard-hearted, and to forgive when we deserve punishment, look with compassion on this thy *son* in *his* time of trouble; restore the guilty, shield and sustain the innocent, walk with those who are appointed to die. Bless those we love and who love us, give us readiness for repentance and, if it be thy will, time to serve thee in newness of life; through Jesus Christ our Lord.

*-91- For Blessings on New Enterprises*

Lord, we desire to place ourselves and what we are about to undertake in Thy hands. Guide, direct, and prosper us, we beseech Thee; and if Thou seest that this undertaking will be for Thy glory, grant us good success. Make us and those who act with us to feel that, unless Thy blessing is with us, we cannot succeed, and that, except the Lord build the house, their labour is but lost that build it. Direct us, then, O Lord, in this and all our doings with Thy most gracious favour, and further us with Thy continual help, that in all our works begun, continued, and ended in Thee, we may glorify Thy Name; through Jesus Christ.

### –92– *For Travellers and Those on Holiday*

Grant, O Lord, that we may so enjoy our holiday at this season, that our bodies may be strengthened, our minds renewed, and our energies quickened for the perfect freedom of thy service; through Jesus Christ our Lord.

### –93– *Travellers*

O God, our heavenly Father, who art present in thy power in every place; Preserve, we beseech thee, all who travel by land, by water or by air (especially those for whom our prayers are desired), surround them with thy loving care, protect them from every danger, and bring them in safety to their journey's end; through Jesus Christ our Lord.

### –94– *Travellers by Road*

Almighty God, giver of life and health, guide we beseech Thee, with Thy wisdom all who are striving to save from injury and death the travellers on our roads. Grant to those who drive along our highways consideration for others, and to those who walk on them or play beside them thoughtful caution and care; that so without fear or disaster we all may come safely to our journey's end, by Thy mercy Who carest for us; through Jesus Christ our Lord.

*−95− On Journey*

Eternal and almighty God, who gave thy Son,
the gate and path of heaven, to live among us;
direct us, we beseech thee, in all our journeys
that they may be with thee and to thee, who art
thyself the source, the end, and the way of all
our journeys; through Jesus Christ our Lord.

# IX

## Events

### –96– *Birth of a Child*

Unto thee, O God, we offer our thanksgiving
for the miracle of birth and for the joy of bring-
ing a new life into thy world. Bless, we beseech
thee, this man and this woman; give them wisdom and patience in the nurture of this child
whom we welcome in thy name; through Jesus
Christ our Lord.

### –97– *On the Birth of a Child*

O Lord God, in Whose hands are the issues of
life, we thank Thee for Thy gifts to us at this
time. We thank Thee for the life given, and
the life preserved. And as Thou hast knit together life and love in one fellowship, so we
pray Thee to grant that with this fresh gift of
life to us, there may be given an increase of love
one to another. Grant that the presence of weakness may awaken our tenderness, enable us to
minister to the little one that has been given to
us in all lovingness, wisdom, and fidelity; and
grant that *he* may live as Thy child, and may
serve this generation according to Thy will;
through Jesus Christ our Lord.

*–98– A Birthday Prayer*

O God, our Father, watch with this thy child as *his* days increase; go with *him* as he walks the ways of the world; give *him* a thankful heart, and grant that *he* may find *his* freedom in doing thy will; through Jesus Christ our Lord.

*–99– For a Birthday*

Almighty and everlasting God, our heavenly Father, Who dost watch over us with Thy love and appoint our days, hear our prayer on behalf of *him* who this day completes another year of *his* earthly life. Under Thy gracious guidance grant unto *him* many years of usefulness and service. Bless *him* and keep *him*, O Lord, and make Thy face to shine upon *him;* through Jesus Christ our Lord.

*–100– Blessing a Child*

Bless, O Lord, this thy child, and grant that as *he* grows in age *he* may grow in grace, and evermore serve and glorify thy Holy Name.

*–101– A Child at Baptism*

O God our Father, we thank thee for our child, (*N.*); and as we take *him* to *his* baptism in thy holy Church we pray thee to receive *him* into

the arms of thy love and to keep *him* ever in
thy watchful care. Give us grace to help *him*
grow in grace, both by our own good example and by instruction in the teachings of the
Church, and may *he* remain a faithful soldier
and servant of our Lord Jesus Christ, to *his* life's
end.

## –102– Baptism

O God, who dost teach and nourish those who
are baptized into thy household the Church,
strengthen and enlighten them with the gifts of
thy Spirit, that they may grow in knowledge
and love of thee and of thy Son, Jesus Christ
our Lord.

## –103– A Godparent's Prayer

Heavenly Father, thou hast called me to this
high privilege and responsibility as a Godfather
(mother) for ———. Help me to be worthy of
it, and to do my duty faithfully through the
years to come. Bless ——— and grant that *he*
may become a faithful follower of Christ and a
loyal member of the Church, and that we may
both continue thine for ever, until we come at
last to thine everlasting kingdom; through Jesus
Christ our Lord.

*–104– At the Adoption of a Child*

O God our Father, who makest us thy children by adoption and grace; Give thy blessing, we humbly beseech thee, to this family, who have now bound themselves one to another in thee, that dwelling together in holiness, they may be made perfect in love; through Jesus Christ our Lord, to whom, with thee and the Holy Ghost, be all honour and glory, world without end.

*–105– On the Adoption of a Child*

Our Father, who hast bestowed upon us this great privilege of taking to ourselves as one of our own one of thy little ones, to love and care for, and to bring up in thy faith and fear, grant us, we pray thee, the grace to give to *him* the full measure of our devotion, and to set before *him* always a good example of Christian life. Bless us in our growth together, and may our home be enriched in the simple joys that come of loving and serving one another; through Jesus Christ our Lord.

*–106– For Those Confirmed*

Almighty and everliving God, who hast knit together in one communion and fellowship all those in every place who call upon the name of our Lord Jesus Christ; We heartily thank thee that,

by the guidance of thy Holy Spirit, these thy
servants have been led to dedicate their lives to
thee in Confirmation; and we humbly beseech
thee, O heavenly Father, that through thy grace
both they, and we, may ever continue in this
holy fellowship, and do all such good works as
thou hast prepared for us to walk in; through
the same Jesus Christ our Lord.

### –107– *For Those About to Be Confirmed*

Strengthen, O Lord, we pray Thee, by Thy
Holy Spirit, Thy servants who are now preparing to seek Thy help in the sacred rite of Confirmation; and grant that all they who bear the
Cross upon their foreheads may bear it also in
their hearts, so that bodily confessing Thee before men, they may be found worthy to be numbered among Thy Saints; through Jesus Christ
our Lord.

### –108– *On One Leaving the Home*

O God, Who art in every place beholding the
evil and the good, take into Thine own keeping our dear one now going into the world of
strangers. Give *him* courage, prudence, self-con-
trol. Grant *him* a right judgment in all things.
Raise up for *him* friends, if it be Thy will, and
deliver *him* from the snares and sorrows of loneliness by the power and joy of Thy Presence.
Grant that in every place *he* may find the House

of God and the gate of heaven. Safeguard *him* with the ministry of Thy never-failing Providence, now and always; for the sake of Jesus Christ our Lord.

### –109– *For Those About To Be Married*

O Lord God, giver of life and love, let thy blessing rest upon those whom thou hast drawn together in love. Build thou for them their home. Give them wisdom for life, and discretion in the guidance of their affairs; and may thy fatherly hand ever be over them and thy Holy Spirit ever be with them; through Jesus Christ our Lord.

### –110– *For a Marriage Conference*

O Holy Jesus, who did bless with thy presence the wedding feast at Cana, bless this man and this woman who are preparing to be joined in the bond of marriage. Give them serenity in their hearts, honesty with each other, and devotion to thee, that they may find strength in time of trouble, patience in time of trial, and joy in companionship all their days.

### –111– *At a Wedding Rehearsal*

Behold and bless, we beseech thee O God, these people gathered in thy Name and presence: the bride and the groom, those who attend them,

their families and their friends. Help us to understand and to accept the blessings of thy love, and give us reverent hearts and minds as we assist in the sacrament of Christian union; through Jesus Christ our Lord.

### –112– *A Marriage Blessing*

O Thou, who by Thy presence in Cana of Galilee, didst sanctify the holy estate of matrimony, send Thy blessing upon Thy servants who have this day entered upon this holy estate, and so fill them with all spiritual benediction and grace, that living together in perfect love and holy peace in this world, in the world to come they may obtain life everlasting; through Jesus Christ our Lord.

### –113– *For Those Joined in Matrimony*

Eternal God, we humbly beseech thee favorably to behold these thy servants now (or about to be) joined in wedlock according to thy holy ordinance; and grant that they, seeking first thy kingdom and thy righteousness, may obtain the manifold blessings of thy grace; through Jesus Christ our Lord.

### –114– *For a Married Couple*

O God of love and tenderness and strength, who hast locked our purposes and made us one flesh,

go with us as we walk the ways of the world; bless our home and our love, our comings and our goings; make us worthy of each other's best; comfort us in trouble, sustain us in the hour of self-distrust; help us to deal tenderly with each other's dreams and knit our lives together in the good companionship of thy Son, Jesus Christ our Lord.

## –115– *For a Marriage Anniversary*

Almighty God, who didst institute the holy estate of matrimony for the mutual help and comfort of Thy children: we thank Thee that Thou hast preserved these Thy servants to this hour. We praise Thee for Thy goodness to them in making their union one of love, peace, and happiness, and that through Thy grace they have been enabled to keep the vow and covenant betwixt them made. Protect them, we beseech Thee, through the years to come, and multiply Thy blessings upon them. May they abound together in love and bear together willingly the burdens of life; through Jesus Christ our Lord.

## –116– *In Marriage Counseling*

O God, our Father, who knowest all thy children, help us with thy wisdom to understand ourselves and each other; melt our pride with the warmth of thy redeeming charity and take us back to our days of loving trust, that we may

build again in the good companionship of Jesus
Christ our Lord.

## –117– *For One Lonely After a Divorce*

O God, who art merciful with our weakness and
patient with our pride, help this thy servant, we
beseech thee, in the brokenness of *his* home and
in the loneliness of *his* heart. Give *him* penitence
for *his* wrong choices, thankfulness for thy goodness in the past, and a will to serve thee gladly
in the years that lie ahead; through Jesus Christ
our Lord.

# X

## CHRISTIAN EDUCATION

### –118– For Parents

Almighty God, heavenly Father, who hast
blessed us with the joy and care of children;
Give us light and strength so to train them, that
they may love whatsoever things are true and
lovely and of good report, following the example of their Saviour, Jesus Christ.

### –119– Families and Homes

Almighty Father, from whom every family in
heaven and earth is named: we entreat Thy mercy
for the families of this and every land, for man
and wife and child, and for all who have the
care of children; that by Thy hallowing our
homes may be blessed and our children may
grow up in the knowledge of Thee and of Thy
Son, Jesus Christ our Lord.

### –120– Children and Parents

Heavenly Father, from whom all fatherhood in
heaven and earth is named, bless we beseech
thee, all children, and give to their parents, and
to all in whose charge they may be, thy Spirit

of wisdom and love; so that the home in which they grow up may be to them an image of thy Kingdom, and the care of their parents a likeness of thy love; through Jesus Christ our Lord.

## –121– For Children

O Lord Jesus Christ who dost embrace children with the arms of thy mercy, and dost make them living members of thy Church; Give them grace, we pray thee, to stand fast in thy faith, to obey thy word, and to abide in thy love; that, being made strong by thy Holy Spirit, they may resist temptation and overcome evil, and may rejoice in the life that now is, and dwell with thee in the life that is to come; through thy merits, O merciful Saviour, who with the Father and the Holy Ghost livest and reignest one God, world without end.

## –122– For the Opening of Schools

Bless, we pray thee, O Father, the children and youth of this nation, returning to their schools and colleges. May thy Holy Spirit enlighten their minds, purify their vision, and strengthen their wills; that being taught of thee they may learn to follow in the steps of him who grew in wisdom and stature, and in favor with God and man; through Jesus Christ our Lord.

### *–123– For Religious Education*

Almighty God, our heavenly Father, who has committed to thy holy Church the care and nurture of thy children; Enlighten with thy wisdom those who teach and those who learn, that, rejoicing in the knowledge of thy truth, they may worship thee and serve thee from generation to generation; through Jesus Christ our Lord.

### *–124– Religious Education*

O God, who hast sent thy beloved Son to be unto us the Way, the Truth and the Life; Grant that we, looking unto him, may set forward the teaching power of thy Church, to the nurture of thy children, the increase of thy Kingdom and the glory of thy Son, Jesus Christ our Lord.

### *–125– For a Church School*

O Father of our Lord Jesus Christ, from whom every family in heaven and on earth is named: Grant that, according to the riches of thy glory, thy servants and children in *this School* may be strengthened with power through thy Spirit, that Christ may dwell in their hearts by faith; that they, being rooted and grounded in love, may be strong to apprehend with all the saints what is the breadth and length and height and depth, and to know the love of Christ which

passeth knowledge; that they may be filled with
all thy fulness; through the same Jesus Christ our
Lord.

### –126– *A Young People's Group*

O God, who hast made us in thy image, we give
thee thanks for friends and homes, for youth and
strength, for hopes and dreams; help us to be
honest, to live up to the best we know, and to
grow in the knowledge and love of thy Son our
Saviour Jesus Christ.

### –127– *For College Work*

Guide, we beseech thee, Almighty God, our sons
and daughters in the schools and colleges of this
land; Protect them in danger, enlighten them in
study, kindle them in imagination, confirm them
in usefulness. Bless with wisdom and honesty
those who minister to them in their needs, both
intellectual and spiritual, and bring them close to
thee who art the beginning and ending of all
truth; through Jesus Christ our Lord.

### –128– *For Schools, Colleges, and Universities*

Almighty God, we beseech thee, with thy gracious favour to behold our universities, colleges,
and schools, that knowledge may be increased
among us, and all good learning flourish and
abound. Bless all who teach and all who learn;

and grant that in humility of heart they may ever look unto thee, who art the fountain of all wisdom; through Jesus Christ our Lord.

## –129– Teachers and Students

Grant, O Lord, to all teachers and students to know that which is worth knowing, to love that which is worth loving, to praise that which pleaseth Thee most, to esteem that which is most precious to Thee, and to dislike whatsoever is evil in Thine eyes. Grant them with true judgment to distinguish things that differ, and above all to search out and to do what is well-pleasing unto Thee, to desire Thee with a whole heart; so desiring Thee, to find Thee; so finding, to love Thee; so loving, to rejoice in Thee.

## –130– For Foreign Students

O God, the Father of all mankind, we remember before thee those who come from many lands to study in our schools and universities. Guide and protect them in the difficulties and temptations which beset them in their new surroundings. Keep alive in their hearts the love of all that is good in their life at home, and give them insight to appreciate and share that which is good in ours. Pardon the faults of temper and manners by which we so often offend them; and grant unto us true humility, love, and patience, that we may welcome them in the spirit of the Master

whom we desire to serve, thy Son, Jesus Christ our Lord.

### –131– *For a Conference Group*

Grant, O Lord, we pray thee, that as we seek for truth we may find that the search leads us to thyself. Give us courage to seek honestly and reverence to seek humbly; and when our minds are perplexed, and we cannot find thee, give us patience and light to go on with our work until at length we come into thy Presence; through Jesus Christ our Lord.

### –132– *For a Conference*

O God, bless to us what we have learned in our fellowship, that we may bring forth in our lives the fruits of Christian truth and love. Confirm us in our renewed resolve to love Thee more and serve Thee better; and may Thy Spirit so move us that henceforth it may be the work of our lives to obey Thee, the joy of our souls to please Thee, and, at the last, the fulfillment of all our desires to dwell with Thee in Thy holy and everlasting kingdom; through Jesus Christ our Lord.

### –133– *For a Clergy Conference*

O Lord Jesus Christ, Head of the Church which is thy Body, by whom we have been chosen as ambassadors and ministers of reconciliation, di-

rect us, we beseech thee, in all our doings with thy most gracious favor; let all our plans and purposes be in accordance with thy holy will, our aim only that we may serve thee and our people faithfully as good shepherds of thy flock. Enlighten us by thy Holy Spirit as we consider together the meaning and obligations of our sacred calling, and the opportunities and responsibilities of the Church in these times. Inspire our minds, assist our wills, and strengthen our hands, that we may not falter or fail in the work thou hast given us to do, to thy honor and glory.

## –134– For Understanding of the Scriptures

Blessed Lord, who hast caused all holy Scriptures to be written for our learning; grant that we may in such wise hear them, read, mark, learn, and inwardly digest them, that by patience and comfort of thy holy Word, we may embrace, and ever hold fast, the blessed hope of everlasting life, which thou hast given us in our Saviour Jesus Christ.

## –135– Before the Bible Reading

O gracious God and most merciful Father, who hast vouchsafed us the rich and precious jewel of thy holy Word: Assist us with thy Spirit that it may be written in our hearts to our everlasting comfort, to reform us, to renew us according to thine own image, to build us up, and edify

us into the perfect building of thy Christ, sanctifying and increasing in us all heavenly virtues. Grant this, O heavenly Father, for Jesus Christ's sake.

## –136– For Students of God's Word

O Almighty God, who has taught us that thy Word is a lantern unto our feet and a light unto our path; grant that we, with all who devoutly read the Holy Scriptures, may realize our fellowship one with another in thee; and may learn thereby to know thee more fully, to love thee more truly, and to follow more faithfully in the steps of thy Son Jesus Christ our Lord; who liveth and reigneth with thee and the Holy Spirit, one God blessed for evermore.

## –137– For Theological Education

Let us pray for theological seminaries:

For all who teach and all who learn, for those who teach each other; for benefactors, for men and women of vision and generosity, for builders; for librarians and caretakers and secretaries and cooks; for all who make it possible for men and women to know and experience and show forth the truth of God.

For Christian homes where the vision of God is first seen in forbearance and forgiveness and thanksgiving.

For all honest pursuit of truth in whatever place.

For Christian parishes where our Lord Jesus Christ is known in darkness and in light, in prayer and word and sacrament, in faith and patience, in the living of our common life in God.

For college chaplains and student workers who minister to growing minds.

For those who labor for our Lord in far off places and against great odds.

O God, who hast preserved thy Church and the true worship of thyself through the fall of empires, the decay of cultures, and the perplexities of reformations, we beseech thee for thy world in which a new age is coming to birth. Keep our spirits alert and hopeful and our wills faithful in whatever tribulations there may be. Help us so to understand our faith that we may pass through critical study to sure conviction. Raise up in our midst scholars who shall be prophets and apostles. Silence the fearful voices of those who would hold us back and preserve us from either impatience or cynicism. Take away our heart of stone and give us a heart of flesh that we may be filled with love of thee; that so thy way may be known upon earth, thy saving health among all nations; through Jesus Christ our Lord.

## –138– For Theological Schools

O God, who through thy Holy Spirit dost illuminate the minds and sanctify the lives of those

whom thou dost call to the work of pastors and
teachers; Look with favor upon all schools for
the instruction and discipline of those who are
to serve in the sacred ministry of thy Church.
Bless those who teach and those who learn, that
they may apply themselves with such diligence
to the knowledge which is able to make men
wise unto salvation, and submit themselves with
such ready obedience to the law of thy Son our
Saviour, that they may fulfill their ministry with
joy; through the same Jesus Christ our Lord.

## –139– For Charity

Let us pray that our fellowship with one another
may be deepened.
By this shall all men know that ye are my disciples, if ye have love one to another.
O God, who hast taught us that all our doings
without charity are nothing worth, forgive us
what is lacking in our fellowship in this (*school*),
for the barriers we have put up between one
another, our lack of sensitiveness to one another's
needs, and our failure to help and encourage one
another. Set us on the right path; grant that we
discern thee in the breaking of the Bread, and
do thou perfect our fellowship in thee, by sending to us the Holy Spirit, the very bond of peace
and of all virtues, who with thee and thy Son
Jesus Christ liveth and reigneth, world without
end.

### –140– *Knowledge of Ourselves*

O God, Inspirer and Teacher of men, who art the truth thou lovest; send out thy light and illumine us. Give us a deep and clear knowledge of ourselves; help us to a growing knowledge of our world; confirm in us the holiness of true reason; strengthen in us the aspiration toward noble and spacious thinking; and in thy good time bring us unto thy holy hill and to thy dwelling; through Jesus Christ our Saviour.

### –141– *For Teachers*

O God, who didst teach the hearts of thy faithful people by sending to them the light of thy Holy Spirit; bless and direct those to whom the office of teacher is committed; give them wisdom to understand the varied scene of life and to see thy purpose as it unfolds; keep their spirits young and fresh that they may understand the aspirations and needs of learners; and so bind teacher and pupil together in a fellowship of discovery that thy presence may be seen in their midst; through Jesus Christ our Lord.

### –142– *A Teacher's Prayer*

O my dear Master, give me a deeper love for the minds of those I teach. Keep me from forcing my

opinions on them. Let me reverence them, and so teach them to reverence themselves.

## –143– *A Private Prayer for Teachers*

Lord Jesus, merciful and patient, grant us grace, I beseech thee, ever to teach in a teachable spirit; learning along with those we teach, and learning from them whenever thou so pleasest. Word of God, speak to us, speak by us, what thou wilt. Wisdom of God, instruct us, instruct by us, if and whom thou wilt. Eternal Truth, reveal thyself to us, reveal thyself by us, in whatsoever measure thou wilt; that we and they may all be taught of God.

# XI

## STUDY

*-144- The Limits of Knowledge*

O Lord, my Maker and Protector, who has graciously sent me into this world, to work out my salvation, enable me to drive from me all such unquiet and perplexing thoughts as may mislead or hinder me in the practice of those duties which thou hast required. When I behold the works of thy hands and consider the course of thy providence, give me Grace always to remember that thy thoughts are not my thoughts, nor thy ways my ways. And while it shall please thee to continue me in this world where much is to be done and little to be known, teach me by thy Holy Spirit to withdraw my mind from unprofitable and dangerous inquiries, from difficulties vainly curious, and doubts impossible to be solved. Let me rejoice in the light which thou hast imparted, let me serve thee with active zeal and humble confidence, and wait with patient expectation for the time in which the soul which thou receivest, shall be satisfied with knowledge. Grant this, O Lord, for Jesus Christ's sake.

## -145- The Study of Religion

Almighty God, our heavenly Father, without whose help labor is useless, without whose light search is vain, invigorate my studies and direct my inquiries, that I may, by due diligence and right discernment establish myself and others in thy holy Faith. Take not, O Lord, thy Holy Spirit from me, let not evil thoughts have dominion in my mind. Let me not linger in ignorance, but enlighten and support me, for the sake of Jesus Christ.

## -146- Before Any New Study

Almighty God, in whose hands are all the powers of man; who givest understanding, and takest it away; who, as it seemeth good unto thee, enlightenest the thoughts of the simple, and darkenest the meditations of the wise, be present with me in my studies and inquiries. Grant, O Lord, that I may not lavish away the life which thou hast given me on useless trifles, nor waste it in vain searches after things which thou hast hidden from me. Enable me, by thy Holy Spirit, so to shun sloth and negligence, that every day may discharge part of the task which thou hast allotted me; and so further with thy help that labour which, without thy help, must be ineffectual, that I may obtain, in all my undertakings, such success as will most promote thy

glory, and the salvation of my own soul, for the sake of Jesus Christ.

## -147- New Learning

In times of doubt and questionings, when our belief is perplexed by new learning, our faith tried by facts too hard for us to grasp and by riddles too deep for us to read, give us still the humility of disciples and the trust of believers. Grant us patience to master the facts, candor to face the issues, insight to penetrate the mysteries, loyalty to truths already known, and courage to welcome new truth yet to be made known.

## -148- The Growth of Knowledge

Almighty God, who hast given us powers which our fathers never knew, to probe thine ancient mysteries, and to discover thy hidden treasures: Quicken our conscience, we beseech thee, as thou dost enlighten our understanding; lest, having tasted the fruits of knowledge, we perish through our own pride and disobedience. We ask it for Jesus Christ's sake.

## -149- Before Preparing a Sermon

O God the Holy Ghost, Who enlightenest the minds of Thy children; send down upon me, I pray Thee, the Spirit of wisdom and understanding, to lead me into all truth, that I may so feed

the flock committed unto me with the words of
eternal life, as with them, to attain unto that
place where, with the Father and the Son, Thou
livest and reignest ever, One God, world without end.

## –150– On Writing Sermons

O Thou in whom peace abides from age to age,
give me now a quiet mind and a listening heart,
that the word which thou wouldest speak in
this church thou mayest make known to me,
and the will which thou wouldest reveal to thy
people here thou mayest lodge in my soul this
day and for evermore; through Jesus Christ our
Lord.

# XII

## Calls

CALLS

tides of quiet compassion for all men. Help
me ... witness to ... the kindness of my
people ... the ... kindness of Thy Son, Jesus
Christ our Lord.

*–151– Before Pastoral Visiting*

Grant, O Lord, I pray, that this day I may go
forth as Thy messenger. Quicken my sympathy
and understanding. Give me Thy comfort for
the sick and sorrowful, Thy cheer for the glad,
Thy love for the lonely, Thy riches for the poor,
Thy peace for the anxious. Make me friendly,
patient, courageous and wise. So use me, I pray,
as to turn many to righteousness; through Jesus
Christ our Lord.

*–152– Before Making a Call*

O Thou who hast Thine own message for those
whom I shall meet this afternoon, give me such
openness toward Thee, that through me Thy
love may be made known, Thy help bestowed,
and the next step for each be made plain; through
Jesus Christ our Lord.

*–153– Before Making Calls*

Be with me, O God, as I make the rounds of my
parish; give me willingness in thy service, patience with my faults, understanding with the

faults of others, compassion for all men. Help me, a sinner, to carry into the homes of my people some of the wholeness of thy Son, Jesus Christ our Lord.

# XIII

## Blessings

### –154– *A Home*

O eternal God, who settest the solitary in families and fillest the hungry with good things, visit this home and family with thy grace and favor; knit them together in thy love through good times and bad, bless their comings in and their goings out, give them thankful hearts for their daily bread and for each other, and bring them at the last into thy heavenly dwelling place; through Jesus Christ our Lord.

### –155– *For a Home*

O Heavenly Father, of whom the whole family in heaven and earth is named; Be present in this house, that all who live here, being kindly affectioned one to another, may find it a haven of blessing and of peace; through Jesus Christ our Lord.

### –156– *For the Family*

Shed the bright rays of thy light, O Father, upon this family and household, that every member of the same, made confident by thy guidance,

may fulfill his daily duty with pure motives and a gallant heart. Be close to us in times of stress and strain, that our courage and our hope may never fail. Let thy sheltering arm protect us, that we may be valiant in all peril. Turn for us sorrow into joy, darkness into sunshine, death into life; so that when the evening comes and our work on earth is done, we may pass triumphantly into the uplands of fellowship in thy family above; through Jesus Christ our Lord.

## –157– This Habitation

Visit, we beseech thee, O Lord this habitation, and drive far from it all snares of the enemy; let thy holy Angels dwell herein to preserve us in peace, and let thy blessing be ever upon us; through Jesus Christ our Lord.

## –158– Blessing of a Home

Our heavenly Father, fill this home with the gladness of Thy presence. Bless all who live here with thy gift of love; help them to show forth thy love to each other and to all men. Keep them safe from all evil and bring them to thy heavenly Kingdom.

## –159– Blessing of a Religious Object

O glorious God, whose perfect beauty the wonderful design of all thy works proclaim; Bless,

we beseech thee, this ———, which we devoutly
offer unto thee, that it may beautify the place
of thy sanctuary and show forth thy glory;
through Jesus Christ our Lord.

## —160— *Blessing of a Cross*

O heavenly Father, who gave thine only-begotten Son both to die for our sins, and to rise again
for our justification; Bless, we beseech thee, this
Cross, that looking upon it with reverence and
true devotion, it may be unto us a sign of triumph, and the banner of our salvation; through
the same Jesus Christ our Lord.

## —161— *Blessing of a Wedding Ring[s]*

Bless, O Lord, this Ring, that he [she] who gives
it and she [he] who wears it may abide in thy
peace, and continue in thy favour, unto their
life's end; through Jesus Christ our Lord.

## —162— *Breaking Ground for a Church*

I break ground for this Church; In the Name of
the Father, and of the Son, and of the Holy
Ghost. Amen.

O Lord God of Israel, who didst move thy
servant David to find out a place for thy temple,
and dost have thy habitation among the sons of

men; Vouchsafe, we beseech thee, to hallow this ground, upon which we propose to build a Church and to set up an Altar therein, that the work now begun may be brought to completion, to the honour and glory of thy Name; through Jesus Christ our Lord.

### –163– *Laying a Church Corner Stone*

I lay this Corner Stone: In the name of the Father, and of the Son, and of the Holy Ghost.

Here let the true faith and fear of God, with brotherly love, ever abide; and may this place now set apart with prayer, and with the invocation and praise of the Most Holy Name, be evermore the Temple of the Most High God; through Jesus Christ our Lord, to whom, with the Father and the Holy Ghost, be all honour and glory, world without end.

### –164– *Building a New Church*

Almighty Father, Who dwellest not in temples made with hands, and yet willest that Thy children shall worship Thee in houses set apart to Thine honour: look graciously, we beseech Thee, upon us whom Thou hast called to build a Church for this parish, that Thou mayest put Thy Name there and hallow it as a witness to generations that are yet to come. Inspire us by

Thy Spirit, that we may lay its foundations in love and set up its pillars with sacrifice. Move the hearts of Thy people to give willingly and to work patiently that this Thy house may be brought to fulfillment in beauty, and that we ourselves may be built up a spiritual temple acceptable unto Thee; through Jesus Christ our Lord.

## –165– Before a Journey or New Undertaking

Lord, we pray thee that thou wilt be with us and keep us as we go upon this journey (or enter upon this new undertaking). Let no change or chance take us out of thy hand; prosper us in our way, and give us grace always to do the things that will please thee.

## –166– For Direction

Direct us, O Lord, in all our doings, with thy most gracious favour, and further us with thy continual help; that in all our works begun, continued, and ended in thee, we may glorify thy holy Name, and finally, by thy mercy, obtain everlasting life; through Jesus Christ our Lord.

## –167– Church Institutions

Vouchsafe, we beseech Thee, merciful Lord, to prosper with Thy blessing all institutions designed for the promotion of Thy glory and the

good of souls. Grant that those who serve Thee in religious houses, hospitals and schools, may set Thy holy will ever before them, and do that which is well-pleasing in Thy sight, and persevere in Thy service unto the end.

## –168– For the Church's Mission

Pour out, we beseech thee, O Lord, thy Spirit upon thy Church, that to all its members may come new visions, new life, new fellowship with Christ, its living Head. Send us out, if thou wilt, and through us send out many another to work for the extension of thy Kingdom throughout the world. Open our hearts that we may receive thy power; open our eyes that we may see Christ with hands outstretched to bless. Do with us what thou wilt and as thou wilt. So shall the earth be filled with the knowledge of thyself as the waters cover the sea. And to thee be the glory and praise, now and for evermore.

## –169– Benedictions

The Peace of God, which passeth all understanding, keep your hearts and minds in the knowledge and love of God, and of his Son Jesus Christ our Lord: And the Blessing of God Almighty, the Father, the Son, and the Holy Ghost, be amongst you, and remain with you always.

The grace of our Lord Jesus Christ, and the love of God, and the fellowship of the Holy Ghost, be with us all evermore.

Unto God's gracious mercy and protection we commit you. The Lord bless you and keep you. The Lord make his face to shine upon you and be gracious unto you. The Lord lift up the light of his countenance upon you, and give you peace, both now and for evermore.

Now unto him who is able to do exceeding abundantly above all that we ask or think according to the power that worketh in us, unto him be glory in the Church and in Christ Jesus throughout all ages, world without end.

Go forth into the world in peace; be of good courage; hold fast that which is good; render to no man evil for evil; strengthen the fainthearted; support the weak; help the afflicted; honor all men. Love and serve the Lord rejoicing in the power of the Holy Spirit. And the blessing of God Almighty, the Father, the Son, and the Holy Ghost be upon you and remain with you for ever.

The God of all grace, who hath called us unto his eternal glory by Christ Jesus, make you per-

fect, stablish, strengthen, settle you. And to him
be glory and dominion for ever and ever.

Peace be with you all that are in Christ Jesus.

Now the God of peace, who brought again
from the dead our Lord Jesus Christ, that great
Shepherd of the sheep, make us perfect in every
work to do his will, working in us that which is
well pleasing in his sight, through Jesus Christ,
to whom be glory for ever and ever.

Now unto him who is able to keep us from falling, and to present us faultless before the presence of his glory, with exceeding joy, to the only
wise God, our Saviour, be glory and majesty,
dominion and power, both now and for ever.

And now may the blessing of the Lord rest and
remain upon all his people in every land of every
tongue. The Lord meet in mercy all that seek
him. The Lord comfort all that suffer and mourn.
The Lord hasten his coming, and now give us
and all his people peace by all means.

God Almighty, bless us with his Holy Spirit;
guard us in our going out and coming in; keep
us ever steadfast in his Faith, free from sin and
safe from danger; through Jesus Christ our Lord.

May the love of the Lord Jesus draw you to himself. May the power of the Lord Jesus strengthen you in his service. May the joy of the Lord Jesus fill your soul.

May the grace of courage, gaiety and quiet mind, with all such blessedness as belongeth to the children of the Father in heaven, be ours, to the praise of the Father, Son and Holy Ghost, who liveth and reigneth one God, world without end.

# XIV

## Trouble

### *–170– For the Desolate*

Have compassion, O most merciful Lord, on all who are lonely and desolate. Be thou their Comforter and Friend; give them such earthly solace as thou seest to be best for them; and bring them to the fuller knowledge of thy love; for the sake of Jesus Christ our Lord.

### *–171– For the Lonely*

Almighty God, look upon those who are lonely and hungry-hearted, the uncompanioned, the unwanted: on all who feel themselves left out and in exile from the joys for which they long. Grant them, O God, some comradeship of understanding and affection; arouse in them an interest or engage them in activity to comfort them in discontent or desolation; and if at times they see that there is no one who would know them, be thou a place for them to flee unto, and cheer them with the welcome of thy love; through Jesus Christ our Lord.

*–172– For the Fearful*

Almighty God, look upon those whose hearts fail them for fear, whose path is dark from overshadowing threats or strewn with obstacles, whose footsteps have well nigh slipped. Deliver them, O God, from every apprehension which is groundless; teach them to trust in the mercies thou bestowest through the changing course of things; let them not feed anxiety or terror with their life-blood, but let them walk in quiet confidence and fortitude, leaning on the staff of thine assistance; through Jesus Christ our Lord.

*–173– For Those Who Have Not Found Love*

O God of Love, who art in all places and times, pour thy spirit of healing and comfort upon every lonely heart. Have pity upon those who are bereft of human love, and on those to whom it has never come. Be unto them a strong consolation, and in the end give them fulness of joy; for the sake of Jesus Christ our Lord.

*–174– For the Gift of Sleep*

O Lord, who hast pity for all our weakness; put from us all worry and all misgiving, that having done our best while it was day, we may, when the night cometh, commit ourselves, our tasks, and all we love into thy keeping, so receiving,

as from thee, the gift of sleep; through Jesus
Christ our Lord.

### –175– *Sleeplessness*

O Holy Jesus, who had no place to lay thy head,
watch with me in the night hours, I beseech thee;
calm my fears and relieve my anxieties with thy
blessed gift of sleep; give me thy peace and grant
that I may wake up refreshed for thy service;
who with the Father and the Holy Spirit rulest
all things.

### –176– *A Person Needing Sleep*

O Heavenly Father, who givest thy children
sleep for the refreshing of their souls and bodies;
Grant this gift to thy servant; keep him in that
perfect peace which thou hast promised to those
whose minds are stayed on thee; inspire him with
a sense of thy presence; so that in the hours of
silence he may enjoy the blessed assurance of
thy love; through Jesus Christ our Lord.

### –177– *For the Despondent*

O God, we beseech thee for all who are weighed
down with the burdens of this world, for whom
there seems little hope; comfort them with the
assurance of thy love, give them some token of
thy continual care for them and, in thy good
time, restore them to a measure of cheerfulness

in the good companionship of Jesus Christ our Lord.

## –178– For the Stricken

Almighty God, look upon those who have been stricken by disaster or a tragic grief, through adversity of circumstance or at the hands of others or by their own unwisdom or misdoing: who eat bread as it were ashes: to whom the morning brings no brightness and the night no rest. Loose them, O God, from the bonds of their imprisonment to misery; lift them from the deep whence their sorrow cries aloud to thee; impart to them the grace of rallying, and console them with the peace which thou hast promised to the souls of men; through Jesus Christ our Lord.

## –179– For Those Who Hallow Suffering

We thank Thee, O Father, for all who hallow suffering; for those who in their thought for others leave no room for pity for themselves; for those whose faith brings light to the dark places of life; and for those whose patience inspires others to hold on. And grant, O loving Father, to all who are bound in the mysterious fellowship of suffering the sense of comradeship with others and the knowledge of Thy love, and give them Thy peace which passes all understanding; through Jesus Christ our Lord.

## *–180– A Person Troubled in Conscience*

O Blessed Lord, the Father of mercies and God of all comfort: We beseech thee look down in pity and compassion on thy servant whose soul is full of trouble. Give *him* a right understanding of *himself*, and also of thy will for *him*, that *he* may neither cast away *his* confidence in thee nor place it anywhere but in thee. Deliver *him* from the fear of evil; lift up the light of thy countenance upon *him*, and give *him* thine everlasting peace; through the merits and mediation of Jesus Christ our Lord.

## *–181– The Nervous*

Regard, O Lord, with thy fatherly compassion, all who are disquieted and tense, who cannot lose themselves either in happy work by day or in restful sleep by night, who looking within do not know themselves and looking to thee do not find thee. Lead them, we pray thee, out of clangor into quietude, out of futility into usefulness, out of despair into the sure serenity of truth. Teach them to believe that thou art faithful, and that thy charity hopeth all things and endureth all things; that all the darkness of the world, even the inner blackness of the soul, cannot quench one small candle of fidelity. Give them of thy perspective, thy humor, thy gift of tranquility and poise. Be so patient with them

that they may learn to be patient with themselves; so firm, that they may lean on thee; so persistent in leading, that they may venture out and find pasture in the sunny fields of thy kingdom, where all who follow thy shepherding may find gladness and delight; in the Name of earth's most calm and daring Son, Word of God, and Master of men, our Saviour Jesus Christ.

## –182– *A Prayer for the Despondent*

Comfort, we beseech thee, most gracious God, this thy servant, cast down and faint of heart amidst the sorrows and difficulties of the world; and grant that, by the power of thy Holy Spirit, *he* may be enabled to go upon *his* way rejoicing, and give thee continual thanks for thy sustaining providence; through Jesus Christ our Lord.

## –183– *For the Needy*

Almighty God, look upon those who are in need but cannot work, or who lack employment and search for it in vain: on those who struggle to meet exacting claims with inadequate resources: on all who move in insecurity, attended by worry or despair. Stand by them, O God, in their deprivations, their dilemmas, and guide them as they try to solve their problems; let them come to open doors of opportunity or refuge; and so quicken and extend the world's concern for all

its people that every man may be ensured a live-
lihood and safety from the bitterness of want;
through Jesus Christ our Lord.

### —184— For the Heavy-Laden

Almighty God, look upon those who are weighed
down by uncongenial or exhausting tasks or by
crippling responsibilities: whose lot is disappointment or frustration, whose freedoms are en-
chained, whose hopes are forfeit. Strengthen
them, O God, for burden-bearing; give them a
gallant spirit for performing all hard duties as
necessity demands; let their load be sometimes
lightened by being shared, if it may not be removed; and refresh them in their heaviness as
thou alone canst do; through Jesus Christ our
Lord.

### —185— An Intercession

Have mercy, O Lord, on all who are homeless,
bereaved, and sorrowful and give them comfort.
Have mercy on all who have none to pray for
them, and none to succour them. Have mercy on
those who have brought punishment and trouble
on themselves, and on those who are dear to
them. Have mercy on all, and give them this
day some token of grace, and some sign of hope;
through Jesus Christ our Lord.

### –186– *For the Faint-Hearted*

O God, who hast made all men, and carest for all alike, have pity on those whose strength seems unequal to the battle of life. Encourage and protect them, and give wisdom and patience to those who are trying to help them; for the sake of Jesus Christ our Lord.

### –187– *For the Handicapped*

O Loving Father, we pray for all who are handicapped in the race of life; the blind, the defective and the delicate, and all who are permanently injured. We pray for those worn with sickness and those who are wasted with misery, for the dying and all unhappy children. May they learn the mystery of the road of suffering which Christ has trodden and the Saints have followed, and bring thee this gift that angels cannot bring, a heart that trusts thee even in the dark; and this we ask in the name of him who himself took our infirmities upon him, even the same Jesus Christ, our Saviour.

### –188– *Faith in Goa*

Almighty God, Lord of the storm and of the calm, the vexed sea and the quiet haven, of day and of night, of life and of death,—grant unto us so to have our hearts stayed upon Thy faith-

fulness, Thine unchangingness and love, that, whatsoever betide us, however black the cloud or dark the night, with quiet faith trusting in Thee we may look upon Thee with untroubled eye, and walking in lowliness towards Thee, and in lovingness towards one another, abide all storms and troubles of this mortal life, beseeching Thee that they may turn to the soul's true good. We ask it for Thy mercy's sake, shown in Jesus Christ our Lord.

### –189– *In Time of Disaster*

Almighty Father, God of Love, we implore thy help in this our great need. If we have neglected thy laws, pardon our carelessness and inspire us to amend our ways. Strengthen the hands of all who minister to the suffering, and make us generous in their support. Have mercy upon all who innocently endure pain or grief. Deal graciously, O God with those who mourn, that they may know the consolation of thy love. May the souls of the departed abide in peace, grow in grace, and rejoice in the everlasting light of thy presence; through thy Son Jesus Christ our Lord.

### –190– *A Steady Hand*

Give, we beseech thee, merciful Lord, to thy waiting people freedom and strength; that we may be loosed from all our fears, and labor with a steady hand; through Jesus Christ our Lord.

### -191- *Inward Calm*

Serene Son of God, whose will subdued the troubled waters and laid to rest the fears of men: Let thy majesty master us, thy power of calm control us; that for our fears we may have faith, and for our disquietude perfect trust in thee; who dost live and govern all things, world without end.

### -192- *Companionship*

Walk thou with us, O Christ, in the way, as thou didst with thy disciples, until the day is spent and our journey done; and then of thy goodness break with us the bread of eternal life, and grant us the vision of thy face; for thy Name's sake, world without end.

### -193- *The Way of the Cross*

Almighty God, whose most dear Son went not up to joy but first he suffered pain, and entered not into glory before he was crucified; Mercifully grant that we, walking in the way of the cross, may find it none other than the way of life and peace; through the same thy Son Jesus Christ our Lord.

*–194– For Quiet Confidence*

O God of peace, who hast taught us that in returning and rest we shall be saved, in quietness
and in confidence shall be our strength; By the
might of thy Spirit lift us, we pray thee, to thy
presence, where we may be still and know that
thou art God; through Jesus Christ our Lord.

# XV

## CONFESSION

–195– *A General Confession*

Almighty and most merciful Father; We have erred, and strayed from thy ways like lost sheep. We have followed too much the devices and desires of our own hearts. We have offended against thy holy laws. We have left undone those things which we ought to have done; And we have done those things which we ought not to have done; And there is no health in us. But thou, O Lord, have mercy upon us, miserable offenders. Spare thou those, O God, who confess their faults. Restore thou those who are penitent; According to thy promises declared unto mankind in Christ Jesus our Lord. And grant, O most merciful Father, for his sake; That we may hereafter live a godly, righteous, and sober life, To the glory of thy holy Name.

–196– *A Confession of Sins*

Forgive me my sins, O Lord—the sins of my present and the sins of my past, the sins of my soul and the sins of my body, the sins which I have done to please myself and the sins which I have done to please others. Forgive me my

casual sins and my deliberate sins and those which
I have laboured so to hide that I have hidden
them even from myself. Forgive me them, O
Lord, forgive them all; for Jesus Christ's sake.

### –197– Before Listening

Help me, O God, to listen to this thy child.
Help me to hear what is said and what is un-
said. Help me to be fair-minded, honest, just and
loving, that the truth may be spoken and received; through Jesus Christ our Lord.

### –198– Before Hearing a Confession

O good Lord Jesus, who came to bear our sins,
help me, a sinner, to be the minister of thy grace
to this thy child; give me patience, wisdom, honesty and compassion, that I may hear and judge
rightly in thy Name, who with the Father and
the Holy Spirit, art God for ever and ever.

### –199– In Counseling

O Lord Jesus Christ, Who didst come to seek
and to save that which was lost, and Who hast
committed to us the ministry of reconciliation,
give me a discerning spirit to judge and advise
aright. Grant that I may never make sad the
hearts that Thou wouldst not have saddened; nor,
healing slightly the hurt of Thy people, speak
peace where there is no peace; but may faithfully and lovingly, firmly and considerately lead

those who seek my help in the paths of truth and peace; for Thy mercies' sake.

## −200− *Our Imperfect Service*

Accept O Lord the imperfect service which we have rendered to thee during the past week (*or* term). Thou knowest all our idle, trifling and uncharitable words; all our wasted, half-employed and misused hours; all our selfishness, vanity, and ungodliness; all our omitted duties and all our committed sins; thou, O Lord, knowest all, rememberest all and must bring all into judgment, even every secret thing. Suffer us not to cloak or veil before thee our hearts or our lives, but forgive, O God, all that thou hast seen amiss in us, for the sake of him who came into the world to save sinners, Jesus Christ our Lord.

## −201− *Need for Forgiveness*

O God, while I am yet a great way off, thou comest to meet me, to take me to thy heart and bring me to thy house and to thy table.

O God, prepare me for reunion with thy love, for I have sinned against thee and am not worthy to be called thy son.

O God, forgive me for not giving thee thy rightful place in my life.

O God, forgive me for caring too much about myself and too little about my brethren.

O God, forgive me for any conduct by which I have done some ill to others or failed to do for them some good I could have done.

O God, forgive me for any prejudice or faulty reasoning by which I have departed from thy truth.

O God, forgive me for any choice of ease or pleasure, or plain neglect of duty, by which I have set aside thy will.

Forgive me, O Father, forgive me all my sins for Jesus' sake, and let me grow in sonship through his grace.

*–202– Confession and Absolution*

LET US JOIN IN A GENERAL CONFESSION

We confess to God Almighty, the Father, the Son, and the Holy Spirit, that we have sinned exceedingly in thought, word, deed, and omission, through our fault, through our own fault, through our own great fault; therefore we pray

God to have mercy upon us and bring us to
everlasting life.

(THEN SHALL THE READER SAY)

May the Almighty and merciful Lord grant us
forgiveness of our sins, time for repentance,
amendment of life, and the grace and comfort
of his Holy Spirit.

*–203– Confession and Absolution*

I confess to God Almighty, the Father, the Son,
and the Holy Ghost, before the whole Company
of Heaven, that I have sinned exceedingly in
thought, word, deed and omission, by my fault,
my own fault, my own most grievous fault:
especially I accuse myself of the following
sins . . .

(HERE FOLLOWS THE CONFESSION)

for these, and all my other sins which I cannot
now remember, or know not of, I am heartily
sorry and firmly purpose amendment.*

*-204– Pardon and Peace*

Grant, we beseech thee, merciful Lord, to thy
faithful people pardon and peace, that they may
be cleansed from all their sins, and serve thee

---

* If the confession is made before a priest, this sentence
should be added: And ask for penance, counsel, and absolution.

with a quiet mind; through Jesus Christ our Lord.

### –205– *Our Failures*

We confess unto Thee, O heavenly Father, as Thy children and Thy people, our hardness, and indifference, and impenitence; our grievous failures in Thy faith and in pure and holy living; our trust in riches, and our misuse of them, our confidence in self, whereby we daily multiply our own temptations. We confess our timorousness as Thy Church and witness before the world, and the sin and bitterness that every man knows in his own heart. Give us all contrition and meekness of heart, O Father, grace to amend our sinful life, and the holy comfort of Thy Spirit to overcome and heal all our evils; through Jesus Christ our Lord.

### –206– *For True Repentance*

Lord give me the repentance which is of the will, that, not only in desire but also in intention and effort I may embrace what is good, especially those virtues which once I neglected or refused, and so be endued with power to accept thy pardon; through Jesus Christ our only Mediator and Advocate.

# XVI

## Forgiveness

### –207– *Pardon and Renewal*

Blot out, we humbly beseech Thee, O Lord, our past transgression; forgive our negligence and ignorance; help us to amend our mistakes and to repair our misunderstanding; and so uplift our hearts in new love and dedication, that we may be unburdened from the grief and shame of past faithlessness, and go forth to serve Thee with renewed courage and devotion; through Jesus Christ our Lord.

### –208– *Pardon*

Lord, for Thy tender mercies' sake, lay not our sins to our charge, but forgive that is past, and give us grace to amend our lives; to decline from sin and incline to virtue, that we may walk with a perfect heart before Thee, now and evermore.

### –209– *For Honesty*

Almighty God, who lookest upon the inward man, forbid us in thy presence the vain endeavor to hide from thee what we have thought and done and truly are. Give us candor to acknowl-

edge freely to thee what must be forever hidden
from the knowledge of others, and may no false
shame keep us from confessing those sins which
no proper shame kept us from committing;
through Jesus Christ our Lord.

### –210– Forgiveness

Lord, of Thy great goodness I beseech Thee
give me true repentance, and forgive me all my
sins, negligences, and ignorances, and endue me
with the grace of Thy Holy Spirit, that I may
amend my life according to Thy holy Word.

### –211– Absolution of Sinners

Our Lord Jesus Christ, who hath left power to
His Church to absolve all sinners who truly repent and believe in Him, of His great mercy
forgive thee thine offenses: And by His authority committed unto me, I absolve thee from all
thy sins in the Name of the Father, and of the
Son, and of the Holy Ghost. Amen. The blessing of God Almighty, the Father, the Son, and
the Holy Ghost, be upon thee and remain with
thee always. Amen. Go in peace; the Lord hath
put away from thee all thy sins.

### –212– Pardon and Absolution

May the good that thou hast done and the evil
that thou hast endured, together with the Pas-

sion of our Lord Jesus Christ, be unto thee for the forgiveness of thy sins. By virtue of the authority committed unto me, I pronounce the pardon and absolution of all thy sins, in the Name of the Father, and of the Son, and of the Holy Ghost. Amen. Depart in peace for God hath put away all thy sins and forget not to pray for me who am also a sinner.

## –213– Remission of Sins

O Lord God of the salvation of thy servants, merciful, gracious, and long-suffering, who repenteth thee of the evil, and willeth not the death of a sinner, but rather that he should be converted and live: Forgive now, O Lord, this thy servant; grant him the assurance of repentance, pardon and remission of his sins, and absolve him from all his offences, voluntary and involuntary; reconcile him and unite him to thy holy Church through Jesus Christ our Lord, with whom be power and glory ascribed unto thee, now and for ever, even unto ages of ages.

## –214– Forgiveness of Sins

Almighty God, our heavenly Father, who of his great mercy hath promised forgiveness of sins to all those who with hearty repentance and true faith turn unto him; Have mercy upon you; pardon and deliver you from all your sins; confirm and strengthen you in all goodness; and

bring you to everlasting life; through Jesus Christ
our Lord.

### –215– Declaration of Pardon

Almighty God, the Father of our Lord Jesus
Christ, who desireth not the death of a sinner,
but rather that he may turn from his wickedness
and live, hath given power, and commandment,
to his Ministers, to declare and pronounce to his
people, being penitent, the Absolution and Remission of their sins. He pardoneth and absolveth
all those who truly repent, and unfeignedly believe his holy Gospel.

Wherefore let us beseech him to grant us true
repentance, and his Holy Spirit, that those things
may please him which we do at this present; and
that the rest of our life hereafter may be pure
and holy; so that at the last we may come to
his eternal joy; through Jesus Christ our Lord.

### –216– An Absolution

The Almighty and merciful Lord grant you Absolution and Remission of all your sins, true repentance, amendment of life, and the grace and
consolation of his Holy Spirit.

# XVII

## Older People

–217– *Abide with Us*

Abide with us, O Lord, for it is toward evening and the day is far spent; abide with us, and with Thy whole Church. Abide with us in the evening of the day, in the evening of life, in the evening of the world. Abide with us in Thy grace and mercy, in holy Word and Sacrament, in Thy comfort and Thy blessing. Abide with us in the night of distress and fear, in the night of doubt and temptation, in the night of bitter death, when these shall overtake us. Abide with us and all Thy faithful ones, O Lord, in time and in eternity.

–218– *The Sea of Life*

Blessed are all Thy saints, O God and King, who have travelled over the tempestuous sea of this life and have made the harbour of peace and felicity. Watch over us who are still on dangerous voyage; and remember such as lie exposed to the rough storms of trouble and temptations. Frail is our vessel, and the ocean is wide; but as in thy mercy Thou hast set our course, so steer the vessel of our life towards the everlast-

ing shore of peace, and bring us at length to the
quiet haven of our heart's desire, where Thou,
O God, art blessed and livest and reignest for
ever.

### –219– *Light at Evening Time*

We commit to thy care, O Lord, those who are
old and full of years, and can no longer bear
the burden and heat of the day. Grant them to
have so trusted and learned of thee in years which
are gone, that in the loss of their daily work and
the world they have long known, they shall not
have lost thee. Vouchsafe to them light at evening time, and the assurance that by serene example they may also serve who only stand and
wait; through Jesus Christ our Lord.

### –220– *Serenity*

God grant me
The serenity to accept the things I cannot
    change,
The courage to change the things I can,
And the wisdom to distinguish the one from the
    other.

### –221– *The Gate of Heaven*

Bring us, O Lord, at our last awakening into
the house and gate of heaven, to enter into that
gate and dwell in that house, where there shall

be no darkness nor dazzling, but one equal light;
no noise nor silence, but one equal music; no
fears nor hopes, but one equal possession; no
ends nor beginnings, but one equal eternity; in
the habitations of Thy glory and dominion world
without end.

## –222– *The Aged and Infirm*

Remember, O Lord, the aged and infirm, those
who feel their life's work is done and can no
longer lend a helping hand where once they did;
all who are passing through the valley of shadows, that they may find that Christ the risen of
the dead is with them, and that there is light at
evening time.

O God our Father, hear our intercessions, answer them according to thy will, and make us
channels of thine infinite pity and love, for the
sake of Jesus Christ thy Son, our Saviour and
Redeemer.

## –223– *Our Loved Ones*

O Heavenly Father, who hast bestowed upon us
the comfort of friends, look lovingly upon our
dear ones from whom we are separated. Protect
and keep them from all harm; prosper and bless
them in all things good. Give them the strength
and consolation of companionship with thee,

who art ever near to those who put their trust
in thee; and grant in thine own good time that
we may renew the fellowship of sight and hand;
through Jesus Christ our Lord.

### –224– *Those We Love*

O God, whose fatherly care reacheth to the ut-
termost parts of the earth; We humbly beseech
thee graciously to behold and bless those whom
we love, now absent from us. Defend them from
all dangers of soul and body; and grant that both
they and we, drawing nearer to thee, may be
bound together by thy love in the communion
of thy Holy Spirit, and in the fellowship of thy
saints; through Jesus Christ our Lord.

### –225– *Old and Young*

O God, Who dost turn the hearts of the fathers
unto the children, and hast granted unto youth
to see visions and to age to dream dreams: we
beseech Thee to draw together the old and the
young, that in fellowship with Thee thy may
understand and help one another, and in Thy
service find their perfect freedom; through Jesus
Christ our Lord.

### –226– *The Swift and Solemn Trust of Life*

O Eternal God, who committest to us the swift
and solemn trust of life; Since we know not

what a day may bring forth, but only that the hour for serving Thee is ever present, may we wake to the instant claims of Thy holy will, not waiting for tomorrow, but yielding today. Lay to rest, by the persuasion of Thy Spirit, the resistance of our passion, our indolence, or our fear. Consecrate with Thy presence the way in which our feet may go, so that the humblest work may shine and the rough places may be made plain. Lift us above unrighteous anger and mistrust, into faith, and hope, and charity. In all things draw us close to our Saviour Christ, that Thy lost image may be traced in us again, and all men, looking at us, may know that we have been with Thee; Through Jesus Christ our Lord.

## –227– *Christ with Us*

Jesus, our Master, do thou meet us while we walk in the way and long to reach the heavenly country; so that, following thy light, we may keep the way of righteousness, and never wander away into the darkness of this world's night, while thou, who art the Way, the Truth, and the Light art shining within us; for thy mercy's sake.

## –228– *A Mind Forgetful of Ill Will*

O God of love who through thine only-begotten Son hast given us a new commandment, that we should love one another even as thou didst

love us, the unworthy and wandering: We pray
thee give to us thy servants, in all the time of
our life on earth, a mind forgetful of past ill
will, a pure conscience and a heart to love our
brethren; through the same thy Son our Saviour
Jesus Christ.

### –229– *For Patience*

Take from us, O God, all tediousness of spirit,
all impatience and unquietness. Let us possess
ourselves in patience; through Jesus Christ our
Lord.

### –230– *Near the End of Life*

Eternal Father, who alone canst control the days
that are gone and the deeds that are done, remove from my burdened memory the weight of
past years, that being set free both from the
glamor of complacency and the palsy of re-
morse, I may reach forth unto those things which
are before and press toward the mark for the
prize of the high calling of God in Christ Jesus.

### –231– *For Those Advanced in Years*

Heavenly Father, whose gift is length of days;
Help us to make noble use of mind and body
in our advancing years.

As thou hast pardoned our transgressions, sift the
ingatherings of our memory that evil may grow
dim and good may shine forth. We bless thee
for thy gifts, especially for thy presence, and
the love of friends in heaven and earth. Grant
us new ties of friendship, new opportunities of
service, joy in the growth and happiness of children, sympathy with those who bear the world's
burdens, clear thought and quiet faith. Teach us
to bear infirmities with cheerful patience. Keep
us from narrow pride in outgrown ways, blind
eyes that will not see the good of change, impatient judgments of the methods and experi-
ments of others.

Let thy peace rule our spirits through all the
trial of our waning powers. Take from us all
fear of death, and all despair or undue love of
life, that with glad hearts at rest in thee we
may await thy will concerning us; through Jesus
Christ our Lord.

## –232– *For Confidence in God*

O Lord God, in whom we live and move and
have our being, open our eyes that we may behold thy Fatherly presence ever about us. Teach
us to be anxious for nothing, and when we have
done what thou hast given us to do, help us,
O God our Saviour, to leave the issue to thy

wisdom, knowing that all things are possible to us through thy Son our Saviour, Jesus Christ.

### -233- *Temporal and Eternal*

O God, the protector of all that trust in thee, without whom nothing is strong, nothing is holy; Increase and multiply upon us thy mercy; that, thou being our ruler and guide, we may so pass through things temporal, that we finally lose not the things eternal. Grant this, O heavenly Father, for the sake of Jesus Christ our Lord.

### -234- *Trust*

O God, the strength of those who walk with thee, without whom nothing is safe, nothing is tranquil; Confirm in us the knowledge of thy presence, that, thou being our companion in the way, we may so deal with our anxieties that at length our hearts may find their rest in thee; through Jesus Christ our Lord.

### -235- *Mercy and Forgiveness*

Almighty and everlasting God, who art always more ready to hear than we to pray, and art wont to give more than either we desire or deserve; Pour down upon us the abundance of thy mercy; forgiving us those things whereof our conscience is afraid, and giving us those good things which we are not worthy to ask, but

through the merits and mediation of Jesus Christ, thy Son, our Lord.

## -236- *Companionship*

Walk thou with us, O Christ, in the way, as thou didst with thy disciples, until the day is spent and our journey done; then of thy goodness break with us the bread of eternal life, and grant us the vision of thy face; for thy Name's sake, world without end.

# XVIII

## SICKNESS

### –237– *For the Sick*

O Lord, holy Father, by whose loving-kindness our souls and bodies are renewed; mercifully look upon this thy servant, that, every cause of sickness being removed, *he* may be restored to soundness of health; through Jesus Christ our Lord.

### –238– *For the Sick*

Almighty God, look upon those who are sick in body or in mind: on the handicapped and the infirm; on all who suffer pain. Bless, O God, the ministrations of every one who gives them care; let thy healing power be their invigoration, to restore them to health or alleviate their ills; let thy loving-kindness be their solace; and grant them the faith, the patience and the valor by which the spirit serves the flesh and abides unconquered; through Jesus Christ our Lord.

### –239– *God's Watchfulness*

Watch thou, dear Lord, with those who wake, or watch, or weep to-night, and give thine an-

gels charge over those who sleep. Tend thy sick ones, O Lord Christ; rest thy weary ones; bless thy dying ones. Soothe thy suffering ones; shield thy joyous ones; and all for thy Love's sake.

### –240– Sick Persons

Almighty Father, giver of life and health: Look mercifully, we beseech thee, on the sick and suffering, especially those for whom our prayers are desired; that, by thy blessing upon them and upon those who minister to them, they may be restored, if it be thy gracious will, to health of body and mind, and give thanks to thee in thy holy Church; through Jesus Christ our Lord.

### –241– A Sick Person

Almighty, everliving God, maker of all mankind: We beseech thee to have mercy upon this thy servant in his affliction. Give him grace to take his sickness with patience and courage; and grant that, if it be thy gracious will, he may recover his bodily health, and serve thee henceforth in newness of life; through Jesus Christ our Lord.

### –242– In Time of Sickness

O God, who knowest the needs of all thy children, look with compassion upon thy sick (*servant, child*) for whom our prayers are offered; give him courage and confidence; bless those who

minister to him of thy healing gifts and, if it
be thy gracious will, restore him to that perfect
health which is thine alone to give; through Jesus
Christ our Lord.

### –243– *For One Who Has Had a Heart Attack*

O God, giver of life and health, hope and courage, watch with this thy servant in *his* anxiety
and helplessness. Bless those whom *he* loves and
those who love *him;* guide those who minister
to *him* in *his* weakness; give him patience and
trust that *he* may be restored to serve thee with
gladness; through Jesus Christ our Lord.

### –244– *For Sufferers*

O Lord, who dost feel the pain of the world,
and lookest upon all sick and suffering persons,
enfolding them with thy love; Grant that in the
midst of pain they may find thy presence; to
doctors and nurses grant tender hearts and healing hands; and give health again in body and
soul, for thy tender mercy's sake.

### –245– *For a Sick Child*

O Heavenly Father, watch with us, we pray
thee, over the sick *child* for whom our prayers
are offered, and grant that *he* may be restored
to that perfect health which it is thine alone to
give; through Jesus Christ our Lord.

### –246– *A Sick Child*

Almighty and merciful God, giver of all power and peace; Watch with us, we pray thee, over this thy child; walk with *him* through the valley of sickness, and lead *him* forth beside the waters of comfort; that, patiently trusting in thy loving-kindness, *he* may rejoice in thy presence all the days of *his* life; through Jesus Christ our Lord.

### –247– *A Sick Child*

O Lord Jesus Christ, Good Shepherd of the sheep, who dost gather the lambs with thine arms, and carry them in thy bosom: We commit into thy loving hands this child. Relieve *his* pain, guard *him* from all danger, restore unto *him* thy gifts of gladness and strength, and raise *him* up to a life of service to thee. Hear us, we beseech thee, for thy dear Name's sake.

### –248– *For the Parents of a Retarded Child*

O God of mercy and compassion, behold and bless these people in their need; fold their child in the arms of thy love; take away all bitterness from their hearts and give them patience, kindness, and wisdom to choose wisely for their child who is a whole person in thy sight; in the name of Jesus Christ our Saviour.

### -249- In Illness

O Lord and heavenly Father, in Whom we live
and move and have our being: grant to me Thy
servant grace to desire only Thy most holy will;
that whether living or dying I may be Thine;
for His sake Who loved us and gave Himself
for us, Jesus Christ our Lord.

### -250- Before an Operation

Almighty God, our heavenly Father, we beseech
thee graciously to comfort thy servant in his suffering, and to bless the means made use of for
his cure. Fill his heart with confidence, that,
though he be sometime afraid, yet he may put
his trust in thee; through Jesus Christ our Lord.

### -251- Before an Operation

Father of compassion and mercy, who never
failest to help and comfort those who cry to
thee for succour; Give strength and courage to
this thy *son* in *his* hour of need. Hold thou
*him* up and he shall be safe; enable *him* to feel
that thou art near, and to know that underneath
are the everlasting arms; grant that, resting on
thy protection, *he* may fear no evil, since thou
art with *him* and wilt comfort *him;* through
Jesus Christ our Saviour.

### −252− *Before an Operation*

Strengthen me, I beseech thee O God, to do
what I have to do, to bear what I have to bear,
that accepting thy healing gifts in the skill and
patience of these doctors and nurses, I may be
restored to usefulness in thy world with a thankful heart; through Jesus Christ our Lord.

### −253− *Before an Operation*

Into thy fatherly keeping, O Lord, I commit
my life completely with trust and confidence.
Thou art my dwelling place, and underneath are
thy everlasting arms. To thee I give my body
that thou mayest repair it. May I fall asleep
peacefully in thee. Guard me through the mo-
ments of unconsciousness, guide the hands of the
surgeon that through the wound he must make
there may enter in thy healing power to restore
me to health and strength. I ask this, O Father,
in the name of my Saviour and Redeemer, Jesus
Christ.

### −254− *Reverie Before an Operation*

Who is so safe as he that is cared for wholly
by God? The schemes and activities of our waking hours plunge us into multitudinous dangers.
Then comes the night when our hands are folded
and we leave it to God's vigilance to keep us

from harm. Not only does He protect us, but while we sleep He instills new life into our veins, so that when we awake we are new creatures. Self-protection involves exhaustion; God's protection brings refreshment. He is safest who is altogether in God's hands.

I am about to surrender my body to His keeping, giving up my consciousness that He may better do His work. I give back my body to its Creator that He may repair it. It is He that will draw the merciful ether veil across my eyes. It is He who will guide the surgeon's knife and open a saving wound through which will rush a tide of healing.

## –255– *For the Surgeon*

Dear Lord, our Great Physician, who in thy earthly walk didst heal the diseases of our frail bodies: Bless the surgeon who shall soon minister to me, thy servant, with knowledge and skill, and guide his hand; so that all things may work together for good, and I be speedily restored to health; who livest and reignest with the Father and the Holy Ghost, One God, world without end.

## –256– *In Pain*

O Lord Jesus Christ, who by thy patience under suffering didst hallow earthly pain and give

us an example of holy obedience to the Father's will: Be near me, I pray thee, in the hours of weakness and pain; sustain me by thy grace that my strength and courage fail not; grant me patience and heal me, if it be thy will; and help me ever to believe that what may befall the body is of little moment if thou hold my soul in life, O my Lord and Saviour, who livest and reignest with the Father and the Holy Ghost, ever One God, world without end.

## –257– *Use of Pain*

We ask thee not, O Lord, to rid us of pain; but grant in thy mercy that our pain may be free from waste, unfretted by rebellion against thy will, unsoiled by thought of ourselves, purified by love of our kind and ennobled by devotion to thy Kingdom; through the merits of thine only Son, our Lord.

## –258– *For Those in Pain*

Breathe down, O Lord, upon all those who are bearing pain, thy spirit of healing, thy spirit of life, thy spirit of peace and hope, of love and joy, thy spirit of courage and endurance. Cast out from them the spirit of anxiety and fear; grant them perfect confidence and trust in thee, that in thy light they may see light; through Christ Jesus our Saviour.

#### –259– *The Silence of Christ*

Lord Jesus, who wast silent when men nailed thee to the Cross, and by pain didst triumph over pain: Pour thy Spirit, we beseech thee, on thy servants when they suffer, that in their quietness and courage thou mayest triumph again; who livest and reignest in the glory of the eternal Trinity, God, world without end.

#### –260– *For the Dying*

O Jesus, our Saviour and our Friend, who didst call the weary and heavy laden to come to thee for rest; let this thy servant now depart in peace, according to thy word, for *his* eyes have seen thy salvation and *he* has a good hope because of thy Word. Lead *him* forth into the green pastures and beside the still waters of thy love; help *him* to lay *his* hand in thine without fear, knowing in whom *he* has believed, and in thine own good time grant *him* to see the king in his beauty and be found worthy to stand in his presence; through thy merits, O blessed Jesus our Saviour and Redeemer, to whom with the Father and the Holy Ghost be glory and praise, world without end.

#### –261– *For One Who Is Afraid to Die*

O Thou who art God from everlasting to everlasting, look with compassion on this thy child:

Hold *him* in the arms of thy mercy and help
*him* to know that *he* is safe in thy love; free
*him* from fear, that *he* may repent and be saved,
and restore *him* to fellowship with thee in *his*
time and thine eternity; through Jesus Christ
our Lord.

## –262– *For One Dying Outside the Faith*

O God, our Father, who in the Lord Jesus Christ
came to seek and to save the wandering and the
lost, we trust thee to deal graciously with this
thy child; behold and bless those who love *him*
and, if it be thy will, bring *him* home in thy
good time to the ample house of thy love;
through Jesus Christ our Saviour.

## –263– *A Commendation*

Depart, O Christian soul, out of this world,
In the Name of God the Father Almighty who
    created thee.
In the Name of Jesus Christ who redeemed thee.
In the Name of the Holy Ghost who sanctifieth
    thee.
May thy rest be this day in peace, and thy
    dwelling-place in the Paradise of God.

## –264– *A Commendatory Prayer When the Soul Is Departed*

Into thy hands, O merciful Saviour, we commend
the soul of thy servant, now departed from the

body. Acknowledge, we humbly beseech thee,
a sheep of thine own fold, a lamb of thine own
flock, a sinner of thine own redeeming. Receive
*him* into the arms of thy mercy, into the blessed
rest of everlasting peace, and into the glorious
company of the saints in light.

### –265– *For One Who Wants to Die*

O God, our Father, who hast made us for thyself, behold and bless this thy servant in *his* distress of mind and body; enfold *him* tenderly in
the arms of thy mercy, give *him* patience to do
thy will and, in thy good time, take *him* into
thy holy keeping; through Jesus Christ our Lord.

### –266– *For Those in Mental Darkness*

O Heavenly Father, we beseech thee to have
mercy upon all thy children who are living in
mental darkness. Restore them to strength of
mind and cheerfulness of spirit, and give them
health and peace; through Jesus Christ our Lord.

### –267– *A Person Mentally Disturbed*

O Heavenly Father, who in thy love and wisdom
knowest the anxieties and fears of thy children;
whose Son Jesus Christ said to his disciples, It is
I, be not afraid; and to the tempest, Peace, be
still: Grant that this thy servant may be strengthened to cast all his care upon thee, for thou

carest for him. Give him quietness; give him un-
shaken trust; and may the day-spring from on
high guide his feet into the way of peace; through
the same Jesus Christ our Lord.

## –268– *For Those Who Minister to the Mentally Diseased*

O Lord Jesus Christ, who didst marvelously lib-
erate the minds and souls of men from evil possession; Grant a measure of thy power to all who
minister to the mentally diseased. Make them
both strong and tender. Encourage them when
sorely tried and frustrated. Open ever wider
to our knowledge the science both of the cause
and the cure of this evil. Those, for whom as
yet we can find no cure, do thou sustain in thy
mercy until they shall awake up after thy likeness and be satisfied.

## –269– *Prayer for Holy Unction*

As with this visible oil thy body outwardly is
anointed, so our heavenly Father, Almighty God,
grant of his infinite goodness that thy soul may
be inwardly anointed with the Holy Ghost, who
is the Spirit of all strength, comfort, relief, and
gladness; And vouchsafe for his great mercy to
restore unto thee thy bodily health and strength
to serve him; and send thee release from all thy
pains, troubles, and diseases, both of body and
mind.

*–270– Laying On of Hands*

__(NAME)__ , I lay my hands upon you with the prayer that you may reach out for in faith, and accept with courage, that Divine healing which Almighty God makes available to all of us through His son, Jesus Christ.

*–271– The Laying of Hands upon a Sick Person*

O Almighty God, whose blessed Son didst lay his hands upon the sick and healed them: Grant, we beseech thee, to this person, on whom we now lay our hands in his Name, refreshment of spirit, and if it be thy holy will, perfect restoration to health; through the same thy Son Jesus Christ our Lord.

*–272– The Anointing of a Sick Person*

O Almighty God, the giver of every perfect gift: Hear us on behalf of this thy servant, and mercifully grant that by this anointing with hallowed oil he may receive relief from his sickness, cleansing from his sins, and healing both of body and soul; through Jesus Christ our Lord.

*–273– Prayers for the Laying On of Hands*

I lay my hands upon you (+) in the Name of the Father, the Son and the Holy Ghost, beseech-

ing the mercies of our Lord Jesus Christ that He by the power of His indwelling presence may heal all infirmities of body or mind or spirit that you may praise Him and serve Him with a grateful heart and a quick mind. Amen.

O Lord Jesus Christ, who hast promised that wheresoever two or three are gathered together in Thy Name, Thou art in the midst; Open our ears that we may hear Thy gracious voice, and prepare our hearts that we may make intercession according to Thy will; who livest and reignest with the Father and the Holy Spirit, One God, world without end. Amen.

Eternal Lord Christ, who art the strength of all who trust in Thee, we bring into Thy Presence these Thy servants ———— We know not what is best for them, but Thou knowest. Lay Thy healing Hand upon them, we beseech Thee, giving them all that is needful for health of body, mind and soul, to serve and glorify Thee, who livest and reignest with the Father and the Holy Ghost, one God, world without end. Amen.

Let us gather into the presence of Christ all who are suffering at this time all over the world, especially those who have no one to pray for them; and commend them to His love and care.

Lord Jesus, we bring in prayer to Thee every one at this time in weariness or pain upon the face of the earth. Far or near, with us or far from us, Lord we beseech Thee for them—wherever they are, or whosoever they be. What help we would ask for ourselves from Thee, in their position, we pray Thee, O God of all comfort, to give it to them. Take them into Thy loving care and tend them. Be Thou very near to them, and supply all their need. This we ask Thee, trusting in Thy love, who livest and reignest, world without end. Amen.

A BLESSING:

God our heavenly Father keep you always in His love, the Lord Jesus be your constant Companion, the Holy Spirit your never failing Source of all sufficient grace to serve Him. . . .

## —274— A Prayer of Healing

May the Father bless thee, who created all things in the beginning; may the Son of God heal thee; may the Holy Ghost enlighten thee, guard thy body, save thy soul, direct thy thoughts, and bring thee safe to the heavenly country; who liveth and reigneth God, throughout all ages.

## —275— A Prayer for Healing

O Almighty God, who art the giver of all health, and the aid of them that turn to thee for suc-

cour; We entreat thy strength and goodness in behalf of this thy servant, that *he* may be healed of *his* infirmities, to thine honour and glory; through Jesus Christ our Lord.

## –276– *Renewal of Health*

O God, the source of all health: So fill our hearts with faith in thy love, that with calm expectancy we may make room for thy power to possess us, and gracefully accept thy healing; through Jesus Christ our Lord.

## –277– *Teach Us to Pray*

O God, who knowest what we need: Give us thy Holy Spirit to teach us what to ask for, and grace to employ thy gifts in thy service; through Jesus Christ our Lord.

## –278– *Courage*

Fortify us, O God, with the courage which cometh only from thee; that in the midst of all our perils and perplexities we may find that peace which only thou canst give; through Jesus Christ our Lord.

## –279– *One Whose Health Is Improving*

O Lord, whose compassions fail not, and whose mercies are new every morning: We give thee

hearty thanks that it hath pleased thee to give, to this our *brother,* both relief from pain and hope of renewed health. Continue, we beseech thee, in *him,* the good work that thou hast begun; that, daily increasing in bodily strength, and humbly rejoicing in thy goodness, *he* may so order *his* life and conversation as always to think and do such things as shall please thee; through Jesus Christ our Lord.

### –280– *Healing Power*

Almighty God, who didst inspire thy servant Saint Luke the Physician, to set forth in the Gospel the love and healing power of thy Son; Manifest in thy Church the like power and love, to the healing of our bodies and our souls; through the same thy Son Jesus Christ our Lord.

### –281– *For Those Shut-In and Isolated*

We pray thee, Lord, for all who are in isolated places, or by infirmity are confined to home or hospital. Bless to them the word of the Gospel over the air, and grant to them a full and consoling sense of thy presence, that together with us they may be strengthened and uplifted by thy gift of grace.

### –282– *For the Seemingly Incurable*

O Lord, who dost feel the pain of the world; look with mercy, we beseech thee, upon those

who in their sickness and suffering are beyond the reach of human skill. To thee alone belongs the power of life, and these souls are thine. If in the mystery of thy providence it shall be their lot to bear their infirmity to the end, then, Lord, of thy love give them grace to endure bravely, and such an assurance of thy presence with them in it that they may, like their Saviour, be made perfect through suffering.

### -283- For the Blind

Wonderful art thou, O God, in thy merciful guidance of man. We thank thee for thy revelations whereby men of science have prevented many of thy children from a life of darkness, and have restored sight to many threatened with blindness. We thank thee that thou dost still provide compensations for those who can never see by the light of the sun: the vision of touch, the quickening of other perceptions, a greater skill of mind and hand, and above all a cheery temper. Bless them, and continue them in the sure hope of the great day when they shall see thee face to face, through Jesus Christ our Lord.

### -284- For the Hospital

Heavenly Father, we thank thee for this house of healing, for it is a sign of thy tender mercy. Bless the doctors, nurses and all who serve here, and grant them wisdom, skill and patience as they

wait upon thy suffering children. Reward them
with knowing that their work is holy, for they
labor together with thee. Raise up friends for
this place that its work may be maintained to
thy glory; through Jesus Christ our Lord.


## -285- For Nurses

O Good Jesus, who hast said, "Inasmuch as ye
do it unto the least of these my brethren, ye do
it unto me," look upon thy servants who have
been called by thee to tend thy sick and suffering children. Give them patience and tenderness, wisdom and truthfulness, and the special
guidance of thy Holy Spirit in their work, so
that they may faithfully minister to those to
whom thou shalt send them, in thee and for thee,
and may be found worthy, at the last, to receive
thy eternal reward; for thine own merit's sake.


## -286- For Medical Work

Almighty God, whose blessed Son Jesus Christ
went about doing good, and healing all manner
of disease among the people; continue, we beseech thee, this his gracious work among us.
Cheer, heal and sanctify the sick, grant to all
doctors and nurses sympathy and skill, and send
down thy blessing on all who labour to prevent
suffering and to forward thy purpose of love,
through Jesus Christ our Lord.

*-287- For a Hospital and School of Nursing*

Almighty Father, whose power and wisdom uphold the hearts of men, shed thy gracious influence upon this Hospital and School of Nursing, that thy way may be known in its daily life, thy saving health among its people.

To those who here exercise the gifts of administration, grant courage and understanding. Sustain with thy patience all who serve with hand or brain, and give them a true vision of the great enterprise which claims their loyalty.

Sanctify, we pray thee, those whom thou hast called to study and practise the arts of healing, and the prevention of disease and pain. Strengthen them with thy life-giving Spirit, that by their ministry the health of the community may be promoted, and thy creation glorified; in the Name of Jesus Christ our Lord.

*-288- Ministry to the Sick*

Grant, we beseech Thee, O merciful God, to all who minister healing and comfort to the sick and suffering Thy protection in the way of duty, strength and patience, tenderness and love for men, and that they may faithfully serve Thee

in their office for the love of Thee, through Jesus
Christ our Lord.

## –289– Thanksgiving for Health Restored

Almighty and merciful God, the author and
giver of life and health, and all good things: We
most humbly bless thee that thou hast been
pleased to deliver from *his* bodily sickness thy
servant, who now desireth to return thanks unto
thee in the presence of all thy people for thy
great mercies vouchsafed to *him*. Impress *his*
heart with a sense of thy goodness; and grant
*him* grace to devote the residue of *his* life to
thy service, walking before thee in holiness and
righteousness all *his* days; through Jesus Christ
our Lord.

## –290– Thanksgiving for Recovery

O God, source of all health and goodness, we
give thee humble and hearty thanks for the re-
covery of this thy (*child, servant*) from *his* sickness and for the return of strength. Bless all who
have ministered to *him* of thy healing gifts, and
send *him* on his way with a thankful heart and
a cheerful spirit; through Jesus Christ our Lord.

# XIX

## Death

### –291– *Fellowship of the Saints*

O God, whose mercies cannot be numbered;
Accept our prayers on behalf of the soul of thy
servant departed, and grant *him* an entrance into
the land of light and joy, in the fellowship of thy
saints; through Jesus Christ our Lord.

### –292– *Life of Perfect Service*

Remember thy servant, O Lord, according to the
favour which thou bearest unto thy people, and
grant that, increasing in knowledge and love of
thee, *he* may go from strength to strength, in the
life of perfect service, in thy heavenly kingdom;
through Jesus Christ our Lord, who liveth and
reigneth with thee and the Holy Ghost ever, one
God, world without end.

### –293– *For All Souls*

O Eternal Lord God, who holdest all souls in
life; Vouchsafe, we beseech thee, to thy whole
Church in paradise and on earth, thy light and
thy peace; and grant that we, following the good

examples of those who have served thee here and
are now at rest, may at the last enter with them
into thine unending joy; through Jesus Christ
our Lord.

## –294– *For an Anniversary of One Departed*

Almighty God, we remember this day before
thee thy faithful servant [*N*.], and we pray thee
that, having opened to *him* the gates of larger
life, thou wilt receive *him* more and more into
thy joyful service; that *he* may win, with thee
and thy servants everywhere, the eternal victory;
through Jesus Christ our Lord.

## –295– *Those Nearest and Dearest*

O God, who knowest the necessities of all thy
children; we pray thee to have in thy holy keeping those precious souls, nearest and dearest to
us, who have departed this life in thy fear and
love. Provide for all their needs, sustain and
comfort them, protect them from all ill, and
grant them eternal joy in thy service. Give them
peace and rest in thy Presence, and bring them
to that glorious perfection promised to thy
saints; for the sake of him who died for us and
rose again, thy Son, Jesus Christ our Lord.

### –296– *For One Who Has Lost a Child at Birth*

I give thanks unto thee, O Lord God, heavenly Father, through Jesus Christ, thy dear Son, that thou hast been so graciously present with me in all my needs, and even though the heavy burden of sorrow has come so soon upon me still thou dost grant me the comforting assurance that all things work together for good to them that love thee. O most merciful Father, I humbly offer thee my love and trust and tenderly commit the soul of my little one into thy keeping against the day when we shall be united in thy Presence; and I beseech thee, take not the comfort of thy Spirit from me, but grant me grace ever to learn and to do thy will; through Jesus Christ, thy Son, our Lord.

### –297– *Death of a Child*

O God, whose most dear Son did take little children into his arms and bless them; Give us grace, we beseech thee, to entrust the soul of this child to thy never-failing care and love, and bring us all to thy heavenly kingdom; through the same thy Son, Jesus Christ our Lord.

### –298– *"It Is Well with the Child"*

Thou gavest *him* into our arms, O Lord, for a little while. Do thou now take *him* into thine

arms forever. It is well with the child. Blessed
be God, who in His good time will reunite us in
the joy of His Presence; through Jesus Christ
our Lord.

## -299- *Thy Perfect Will*

O Father of all, we pray thee for those whom we
love but see no longer. Grant them thy peace;
let light perpetual shine upon them; and, in thy
loving wisdom and almighty power, work in
them the good purpose of thy perfect will;
through Jesus Christ our Lord.

## -300- *For Those Bereaved by Sudden Death*

O God, our only help in time of need, watch
with these thy people in their time of trouble;
strengthen and quiet them with thy mercy, receive thy servant in *his* sudden death and take
*him* into thy holy keeping; through Jesus Christ
our Lord.

## -301- *For a Suicide*

O God, who knowest all our lights and all our
shadows, look with compassion on this thy child
who has taken *his* life with *his* own hand and
receive him as thine own child. Deal graciously,
we pray thee, with those who love *him*, and
grant that in all their troubles they may know

thy healing and redeeming love, made known to us in Jesus Christ our Lord.

## –302– *The Departed*

Into thy hands, O God, we commend the souls of all our loved ones (*especially* ———) as into the hands of a faithful Creator and most loving Saviour; beseeching Thee to grant unto them pardon and peace and, of Thine infinite goodness, wisdom and power, to work in them the good purpose of Thy perfect will; through Jesus Christ our Lord.

## –303– *Thanksgiving for a Life*

We thank thee, O God, for all the goodness and courage which have passed from the life of this thy servant into the life of others and have left the world richer for his presence—for a life's task faithfully and honourably discharged; for good humour and gracious affection and kindly generosity; for sadness met without surrender, and weakness endured without defeat; through Jesus Christ our Lord.

# XX

## Bereavement

### –304– *For Consolation*

O Heavenly Father, whose blessed Son Jesus
Christ did weep at the grave of Lazarus his
friend: Look, we beseech thee, with compassion
upon those who are now in sorrow and affliction;
comfort them, O Lord, with thy gracious con-
solations; make them to know that all things
work together for good to them that love thee;
and grant them evermore sure trust and confidence in thy fatherly care; through the same
Jesus Christ our Lord.

### –305– *Following in Faith*

O Lord Jesus Christ, who by thy death didst
take away the sting of death; Grant unto us thy
servants so to follow in faith where thou hast
led the way, that we may at length fall asleep
peacefully in thee, and awake up after thy likeness; through thy mercy, who livest with the
Father and the Holy Ghost, one God, world
without end.

## –306– *For Those Who Mourn*

Almighty God, Father of mercies and giver of all comfort; Deal graciously, we pray thee, with all those who mourn, that, casting every care on thee, they may know the consolation of thy love; through Jesus Christ our Lord.

## –307– *For Trustfulness*

O most loving Father, who willest us to give thanks for all things, to dread nothing but the loss of thee, and to cast all our care on thee, who carest for us; Preserve us from faithless fears and worldly anxieties, and grant that no clouds of this mortal life may hide from us the light of that love which is immortal, and which thou hast manifested unto us in thy Son, Jesus Christ our Lord.

## –308– *For Those We Love*

Almighty God, we entrust all who are dear to us to thy never-failing care and love, for this life and the life to come; knowing that thou art doing for them better things than we can desire or pray for; through Jesus Christ our Lord.

## –309– *The Household of Faith*

O thou who art the God of the generations of men, we thank thee for all who have walked

humbly with thee, and especially for those near to us and dear, in whose lives we have seen the vision of thy beauty. May we know that in the body, or out of the body, they are with thee. Make us glad in their living, comfort and teach us through their dying. Unite us still, God of our souls, in one household of faith and love, one family in heaven and upon earth; through Jesus Christ our Lord.

### –310– *For the Bereaved*

Grant, O Lord, to all who are bereaved the spirit of faith and courage, that they may have strength to meet the days to come with steadfastness and patience; not sorrowing as those without hope, but in thankful remembrance of thy great goodness in past years, and in the sure expectation of a joyful reunion with those they love; and this we ask in the Name of Jesus Christ our Saviour.

### –311– *A True Faith*

O Heavenly Father, who hast given us a true faith and a sure hope; Help us, we pray thee, amidst all the things that pass our understanding, to live as those who believe and trust in thy fatherly care, in the communion of saints, the forgiveness of sins, and the resurrection to life everlasting; and strengthen, we beseech thee, this faith and hope in us all the days of our life; through Jesus Christ our Lord.

## –312– *Peace and Comfort*

Blessed Jesus, who hast borne our griefs and carried our sorrows; Satisfy us with thy mercy, and strengthen us with thy might; that, in all our sorrow and desolation, we may find peace in thy Presence, and comfort in thy love; who art our Hope and our Strength, our very present Help in trouble.

## –313– *Absent Friends*

O God, who art present in every place; Mercifully hear our prayers for those whom we love, now absent from us; watch over them, we beseech thee, and protect them in all anxiety, danger and temptation; teach us and them to know that thou art always near, and that we are one in thee for ever; through Jesus Christ our Lord.

## –314– *For the Sorrowing*

O God, who holdest all souls in life: Cleanse our sorrow by thy gift of faith, and confirm in our hearts the knowledge of him who is the Resurrection and the Life, thy Son Jesus Christ our Lord.

## –315– *For All Who Mourn*

In thy boundless compassion, O Lord, console all who mourn. Give to them that faith which

sees in death but the gate to life eternal, so that
with quietude and fearlessness they may continue their course on earth until by thy call they
are united to their loved ones gone before;
through Jesus Christ our Lord.

### –316– *For Mourners*

Lord Jesus, we beseech thee, by the loneliness
of thy suffering on the cross, be nigh unto all
them that are desolate and in pain or sorrow
to-day; and let thy presence transform their
loneliness into comfort, consolation, and holy
fellowship with thee, Lord Jesus, thou pitiful
Saviour.

### –317– *Those Who Mourn*

Comfort, O Lord, we pray thee, all who mourn
for the loss of those near and dear to them; be
with them in their sorrow; give them faith to
look beyond the troubles of the present time,
and to know that neither life nor death can separate us from the love of God which is in Jesus
Christ our Lord.

### –318– *Comfort in Grief*

O God, whose blessed Son on the cross did know
the desolation of loneliness from thee; comfort
these thy servants in their grief and emptiness,

enfold them in the arms of thy mercy and give them peace; through Jesus Christ our Lord.

### –319– *For a Bereaved Person*

O God, I give thee back my loved one and give thee thanks for the years thou didst entrust *him* to my care.

### –320– *For a Peaceful Heart*

Almighty God, who hast taught us that they who mourn shall be comforted; grant that in all our grief we may turn to thee; and, because our need is beyond the help of men, grant us the peace of thy consolation and the joy of thy love; through Jesus Christ our Lord.

### –321– *Before Calling on One Bereaved*

O Thou in whose house are many mansions, speak through me to these, whose loved one has gone from their sight, but not from thine. There is naught in me to heal the wounded heart or fill the aching void. But let thy words of comfort and truth be given me to speak, that these sorrowing ones may find their peace in thee; through Jesus Christ our Lord.

# XXI

## Sundays

### –322– *God's Presence in the Sanctuary*

O Lord, who hast taught us that where thy faithful people are, there art thou in the midst of them; be present, we pray thee, in thy Church's worship, that our prayer and praise may be in thy Name and that all men may know that our fellowship is with the Father and thee, his only Son, to whom, in the unity of the Holy Spirit, be honor and glory, world without end.

### –323– *For the Spirit of Prayer*

O almighty God, who pourest out on all who desire it, the spirit of grace and of supplication; Deliver us, when we draw nigh to thee, from coldness of heart and wanderings of mind, that with steadfast thoughts and kindled affections, we may worship thee in spirit and in truth; through Jesus Christ our Lord.

### –324– *Before Worship*

O Lord Most High, let our prayers be set before thee as incense, and the lifting up of our hands as the evening sacrifice. Unite us in faith with

thy whole Church, in hope with thy saints in heaven, and in love with all who are praying at this hour; and grant by thy mercies, that we may present our bodies a living sacrifice, holy, acceptable unto thee, which is our reasonable service, and by thy grace be enabled to offer unto thee the sacrifice of a contrite heart, which thou, O God, wilt not despise.

*–325– The Lord's Day*

O God, give Thy people grace to use aright Thy holy day; that it may be a day of mercy to the heavy-laden; a day of resurrection to newness of life; a day to worship Thee in the fellowship of the faithful; through Jesus Christ our Lord.

*–326– Before a Service of Worship*

Be with us, O Lord, as we enter thy house, and grant that the thoughts of our hearts may be drawn close to thee; through Jesus Christ our Lord.

*–327– Before a Service of Worship*

Almighty God, our heavenly Father, Whose Son Jesus Christ came to cast fire upon the earth: grant that by the prayers of Thy faithful people a fire of burning zeal may be kindled, and pass from heart to heart, till all our hardness is melted in the warmth of Thy love; through Him Who

loved us and gave Himself for us, Jesus Christ
our Lord.

*–328– Before a Service of Worship*

Almighty God, unto whom all hearts are open,
all desires known, and from whom no secrets are
hid; Cleanse the thoughts of our hearts by the
inspiration of thy Holy Spirit, that we may per-
fectly love thee, and worthily magnify thy holy
Name; through Jesus Christ our Lord.

*–329– Before a Service of Worship*

Open wide the window of our spirits, O Lord,
and fill us full of light; open wide the door of our
hearts, that we may receive and entertain thee
with all our powers of adoration and love.

*–330– Before a Service of Worship*

Open thou our lips, O Lord, and purify our
hearts, that we may offer thee a service worthy
of thy holy Name.

*–331– After a Service of Worship*

Sanctify, O Lord, both our coming in and our
going out; and grant that when we leave thy
house we may not leave thy Presence, but be
thou ever near unto us and keep us near unto
thee, through Jesus Christ our Lord.

## –332– *After a Service of Worship*

O God
in whose will is our peace
preserve us in our going out and coming in,
from this time forth for evermore.

## –333– *After a Service of Worship*

Grant, we beseech thee, merciful Lord, that the words we have said and sung with our lips, we may believe in our hearts, and steadfastly show forth in our lives; through Jesus Christ our Lord.

## –334– *After a Service of Worship*

Grant, O Lord, that as we leave thy house we may not leave thy presence, but walk in thy paths all the days of our life, through Jesus Christ our Lord.

## –335– *After a Service of Worship*

O God, who makest us glad with the weekly remembrance of the glorious resurrection of thy Son our Lord: Vouchsafe us this day such blessing through our worship of thee, that the days to come may be spent in thy service; through the same Jesus Christ our Lord.

## –336– *After a Service of Worship*

Almighty God, who hast given us grace at this time with one accord to make our common supplications unto thee; and dost promise that when two or three are gathered together in thy Name thou wilt grant their requests; Fulfil now, O Lord, the desires and petitions of thy servants, as may be most expedient for them; granting us in this world knowledge of thy truth, and in the world to come life everlasting.

## –337– *After a Service of Worship*

Grant, we beseech thee, Almighty God, that the words which we have heard this day with our outward ears, may, through thy grace, be so grafted inwardly in our hearts, that they may bring forth in us the fruit of good living, to the honour and praise of thy Name; through Jesus Christ our Lord.

## –338– *Before Preaching*

O Lord, Who on the mount didst preach to Thy disciples, enable me, I pray Thee, rightly to deliver Thy message to Thy people. Open their ears, that they may hear the words which belong unto eternal life. Enlighten my mind and grant me simplicity of utterance. Deliver me from the fear of man, and from all self-seeking,

pride and vain-glory. O living Word of God, speak in me and speak by me, to Thy Father's glory, and the salvation and sanctification of Thy people.

### -339- Before Preaching God's Word

O Lord, I humbly place myself before you, for you have made me what I am, and have called me to do what I am trying to do. I have no words to say that have any worth, except those that you give me to say. Help me to hear your words, enable me to speak your words, and help this people to hear them, that the Living Word of Christ may be truly spoken, really heard, and actually grafted in our hearts.

### -340- Before Preaching a Sermon

O God, our Father, who hast called sinful men to speak forth the saving truth of thy holy Gospel, help me now, I beseech thee, to be a faithful messenger to the people thou hast committed to my charge; give me honest conviction, clear speech, and a pure intention, to thy great glory and the salvation of souls; through Jesus Christ our Lord.

### -341- A Prayer Before the Sermon

O God, grant me grace to speak thy word faithfully and without selfish concern. I have tried to

prepare this message for thy children so they may receive the saving life of our Lord. But my efforts have been marred by the desire to win the applause of those who listen. Now in this moment before I speak, turn my thoughts again to the needs of these children and thy will for their lives. Father, I need thy forgiveness if my words are to be thine. Speak through my weakness and pride to the souls of those present, that they may know and receive the saving strength of Jesus Christ our Lord.

### –342– A Private Prayer After Preaching

O Lord God, heavenly Father, I thank thee that thou hast given me the grace and the courage to stand before this people and to try to speak to them thy words. If anything good was said, I thank thee for enabling me to say it; if no good thing was said, I beseech thee to forgive the weakness, the deafness, and the disobedience of thy servant. All honor, glory and majesty be eternally ascribed unto thee, and shown forth in the world through thy holy Church and the lives of all thy faithful people in the Body of Jesus Christ, thy Son, our Lord and Saviour.

### –343– After Preaching

O God, our Father, take these feeble words of mine and make them thine; fill in the gaps of my inadequacy, forgive my pride and error, and

grant that whatever was said in honesty and truth may be used for the upbuilding of thy people and the glory of thy holy Name; through Jesus Christ our Lord.

### -344- *Before the Sermon*

O God, we beseech thee, make us honest money-changers; that in rendering thine eternal Gospel in coin of the present day, we may give full value for that which we have received; through Jesus Christ our Lord.

### -345- *Before the Sermon*

O God, our great companion, lead us day by day deeper into the mystery of thy life and ours, and make us interpreters of life to our fellows.

### -346- *Before the Sermon*

O God, forasmuch as without thee we are not able to please thee; Mercifully grant that thy Holy Spirit may in all things direct and rule our hearts; through Jesus Christ our Lord.

### -347- *Before the Sermon*

O Lord Christ, who, when thine hour was come, didst go without fear among those who sought thy life: Grant us grace to confess thee before

men, without arrogance and without fear, that thy holy name may be glorified.

### –348– *Before the Sermon*

Come, Holy Spirit, come: come as the wind and cleanse; come as the fire and burn; convict, convert, consecrate our lives, to our great good and thy great glory; through Jesus Christ our Lord.

### –349– *Before the Sermon*

Grant, we beseech thee, almighty God, that thy word only may be spoken and thine only received; through Jesus Christ our Lord.

### –350– *Before the Sermon*

Open our hearts, O God, enlighten our minds and kindle our spirits that we may receive and transmit the gift of thy love in Jesus Christ our Lord.

### –351– *After the Sermon*

And now to God the Father, God the Son, God the Holy Ghost be ascribed, as is most justly due, all might, majesty, dominion, power and glory, world without end.

*-352- After the Sermon*

Pardon what we have been, sanctify what we are, order what we shall be, that thine may be the glory and ours the eternal salvation; through Jesus Christ our Lord.

*-353- After the Sermon*

O Most merciful Redeemer, Friend and Brother, may we know Thee more clearly, love Thee more dearly, and follow Thee more nearly; for Thine own sake.

*-354- After the Sermon*

O Thou, who art the light of the minds that know thee, the life of the souls that love thee, and the strength of the wills that serve thee; help us so to know thee that we may truly love thee, so to love thee that we may fully serve thee, whom to serve is perfect freedom; through Jesus Christ our Lord.

*-355- Before the Holy Communion*

O God, who alone canst guide our feet into the sanctuary of thy presence: Make ready, we beseech thee, our hearts to receive the sacrament of that love whereby thy Son hath redeemed us; through Jesus Christ our Lord.

*-356- Before the Holy Communion*

O Lord Jesus Christ, who hast ordained this holy
Sacrament to be a pledge of thy love and a continual remembrance of thy passion: Grant that
we, who partake thereof by faith with thanksgiving, may grow up into thee in all things, until we come to thy eternal joy; who with the
Father and the Holy Ghost livest and reignest,
one God, world without end.

*-357- Before the Holy Communion*

Visit, O Lord, we pray thee, and cleanse our
consciences, that thy Son our Lord Jesus Christ,
when he cometh, may find in us a dwelling prepared for himself; who liveth and reigneth with
thee in the unity of the Spirit, one God, world
without end.

*-358- Before the Holy Communion*

Most gracious God, incline thy merciful ears
unto our prayers, and enlighten our hearts by
the grace of thy Holy Spirit: that we may
worthily serve at thy holy Mysteries, and love
thee with an everlasting love.

*-359- Before the Holy Communion*

Come, Holy Ghost, our souls inspire,
And lighten with celestial fire,

Thou the anointing Spirit art,
Who dost thy sevenfold gifts impart.

Thy blessed unction from above,
Is comfort, life, and fire of love.
Enable with perpetual light
The dulness of our blinded sight.

Anoint and cheer our soiled face
With abundance of thy grace.
Keep far our foes, give peace at home;
Where thou art guide, no ill can come.

Teach us to know the Father, Son,
And thee, of both, to be but One;
That through the ages all along,
This may be our endless song:

> Praise to thy eternal merit,
> Father, Son, and Holy Spirit.

## -360- Before the Holy Communion

Grant, O Father, that when we receive the blessed Sacrament of the Body and Blood of Christ, coming to those holy mysteries in faith, and love, and true repentance, we may receive remission of our sins, and be filled with thy grace and heavenly benediction; through Jesus Christ our Lord.

*–361– Special Intention*

O God, grant that seeking thee I may rejoice in thee; let me not wander from thy presence, nor leave untaken any grace thou willest for me; give ear, I beseech thee, to the special prayer I wish to offer with this Eucharist (*for* –––––), (*that* –––––); and as I ask thy blessing on myself, I ask it likewise on all who pray with me and on thy whole Church; through Jesus Christ our Lord.

*–362– A Short Form of Preparation for the Holy Communion*

O God, thou art my God, I have no good like unto thee: and I desire to come to thee in thy house and at thine altar, to do my bounden duty and service in obedience to Christ's command.

O God, I do not come alone, but as a member of Christ, and with his Church, the household of the faithful: that I, with them: and they, with me and all of us in him may be strengthened for answering thee rightly in our lives.

O God, as I come before thee in thy sanctuary, let me thoughtfully recall thy will: let me give thee honor and receive thy help through Jesus Christ: and let me gratefully resolve to do thy

will better day by day, not trusting in myself
but in thee.

O God, although I have no good like unto thee,
I have forgotten thee more than I have remembered thee; often I have followed my own way:
neither loving thee nor loving others as I should,
nor walking by thy truth, nor with a steady faith
in thee; and with sorrow for my sins of every
kind I ask thy forgiveness for Jesus' sake, that
my soul may be cleansed.

O God, hear the special prayer I wish to bring
thee in this Eucharist, (*for* ————), (*that*
————) and grant, O Lord, above all else, that
we who come to bless thee and be blessed by
thee may be made of one mind in the Church,
thy household, to spread the kingdom of thy
good among men.

O God who knowest me in my best and in my
worst, make clean my heart and turn it toward
thee in loving prayer and praise.

*—363— After the Holy Communion*

Almighty and ever-living God, we most heartily
thank thee that we are very members incorpo-
rate in the mystical body of thy Son, which is
the blessed company of all faithful people. And

we most humbly beseech thee, O heavenly
Father, so to assist us with thy grace, that we
may continue in that holy fellowship, and do
all such good works as thou hast prepared for
us to walk in; through Jesus Christ our Lord.

## –364– After the Holy Communion

O Lord Jesus Christ, who saidst unto thine Apostles, Peace I leave with you, my peace I give
unto you; Regard not our sins, but the faith of
thy Church; and grant to it that peace and unity
which is according to thy will, who livest and
reignest with the Father and the Holy Ghost,
one God, world without end.

## –365– After the Holy Communion

O Lord Jesus Christ, who in a wonderful sacrament has left unto us a memorial of thy passion;
Grant us, we beseech thee, so to venerate the
Sacred Mysteries of thy Body and Blood, that
we may ever perceive within ourselves the fruit
of thy redemption; who livest and reignest with
the Father in the unity of the Holy Spirit, God,
for ever and ever.

## –366– After the Holy Communion

O God, whose blessed Son did manifest himself
to his disciples in the breaking of bread; Open,
we pray thee, the eyes of our faith, that we may

behold thee in all thy works; through the same thy Son Jesus Christ our Lord.

## —367— *After the Holy Communion*

O God, who hast ordained the sacrament of the altar; Grant that with honorable and faithful lives we may guard the holy flame of thy presence, which thou hast given us in these sacred mysteries; through Jesus Christ our Lord.

## —368— *After the Holy Communion*

Remember, O Lord, what thou hast wrought in us, and not what we deserve, and as thou hast called us to thy service, make us worthy of our calling, through Jesus Christ our Lord.

## —369— *After the Holy Communion*

O God our heavenly Father, whose we are, and whom we seek to answer rightly, abide thou within us in the might of thy grace, that we may show forth thy praise not only with our lips, but in our lives, in love and truth and faith; through Jesus Christ our Lord, who liveth and reigneth with thee and the Holy Spirit ever, one God, world without end.

# XXII

## Church (Local)

*–370– For the Parish*

O God, our heavenly Father, graciously behold
this congregation. Bind together its members
with cords of friendliness and sympathy. Give
us the vision of our common duty to Church
and State and make us glad and strong in the
doing of it. By all the memories of a great past,
rouse us to hear the calls of the present. Grant
wisdom, courage and patience to our leaders, and
fill us all with the spirit of loving service; that
whatsoever we do in word or deed may be done
in the Name of the Lord Jesus, through whom
we offer this our prayer.

*–371– True Religion*

O God, Holy Ghost, Sanctifier of the faithful,
visit, we pray thee, this Congregation with thy
love and favour; enlighten their minds more and
more with the light of the everlasting Gospel;
graft in their hearts a love of the truth; increase
in them true religion; nourish them with all
goodness; and of thy great mercy keep them in
the same, O blessed Spirit, whom, with the Father

and the Son together, we worship and glorify as one God, world without end.

### –372– *For Our Parish*

O Almighty and Everlasting God, who dost govern all things in heaven and earth, mercifully hear our prayers, and grant unto us in this Parish and Congregation all things that are needful; strengthen and confirm the faithful; visit and relieve the sick; bless and protect the children; turn and soften the wicked; arouse the careless; recover the fallen; restore the penitent; remove all hindrances to the advancement of thy truth; and bring us all to be of one heart and mind within thy holy Church, to the honor of thy Name; through Jesus Christ our Lord.

### –373– *For Our Parish Church*

O God our Heavenly Father, make the door of our Parish Church wide enough to receive all who need human love and fellowship and a Father's care; and narrow enough to shut out all envy, pride, and uncharitableness. Make its threshold smooth enough to be no stumbling-block to children, to weak or straying feet; but rugged and strong enough to turn back the tempter's power. O Heavenly Father, make the door of our Parish Church a gateway to Thy eternal Kingdom. Bless every member and worker in our Parish. May all that we do be

to Thy Honor and Glory, the upbuilding of
our Parish, and the extension of Thy Kingdom.
May we continue to be Thine forever and daily
increase in Thy Holy Spirit of love and service
to others; through Jesus Christ our Lord and
Saviour.

### –374– *A Parish Prayer*

FATHER of all mankind: We pray that to this
church all thy children may ever be welcome.
Hither may the little children love to come, and
young men and maidens to be strengthened for
the battle of life. Here may the strong renew
their strength and win for their life a noble consecration. And hither may age turn its footsteps
to find the rest of God and light at eventide.

Here may the poor and needy find friends.
Here may the tempted find succor, the sorrowing find comfort, and the bereaved learn that
over their beloved death has no more dominion.

Here may they who fear be encouraged, and
they who doubt have their better trusts and
hopes confirmed.

Here may the careless be awakened to a sense
of their folly and guilt, and to timely repentance.

Here may the oppressed and striving souls be
assured of the mercy that triumphs over sin and
receive help to go on their way rejoicing.

Through our Lord Jesus Christ.

*–375– For the Every Member Canvass*

Prosper, O Lord, our effort to enlist thy children in loving ministry to thy world family. Help us to see that we are unworthy of thy blessings unless we share them with others. May we feel the high privilege of Christian stewardship, and count it joy to aid in speeding thy messengers; through Jesus Christ our Lord.

*–376– For Faithfulness in the Use of This World's Goods*

Almighty God, whose loving hand hath given us all that we possess; Grant us grace that we may honour thee with our substance, and remembering the account which we must one day give, may be faithful stewards of thy bounty; through Jesus Christ our Lord.

*–377– For Proper Stewardship*

Almighty God, the source of all that we can have, and all that we can hope for,

Grant that we may be worthy custodians of the earth in which we dwell.

Make us creative so that we will not burden others;

Make us conservative so that we will not squander what comes our way;

Make us perceptive so that we may properly

weigh our necessities against the needs of
others;

Make us generous so that we may give freely
of what we have that others can enjoy a por-
tion of our fortune.

Remove from us all trust in anything but thee;

Strengthen us in the knowledge that thou wilt
always provide all that we really need;

And finally, by thy Grace, instill in us that perfect desire to be thy servants and ultimately
to be with thee in thy Heavenly Kingdom,

Who reignest forever and ever, Jesus Christ, our
Lord.

## –378– *For Lay Readers*

Look, we beseech Thee, merciful Father, upon
those whom Thou hast called to be readers in
Thy Church; and grant that they may be so
filled with Thy Holy Spirit that, seeking only
Thy glory and the salvation of souls, they may
preach Thy Word with steadfast devotion, and
by the constancy of their faith and the innocency of their lives may adorn the doctrine of
Christ our Saviour in all things; through the same
Jesus Christ our Lord.

## –379– *For a Preaching Mission*

O most loving Father, who hast revealed thyself
to men in the person of thy Son Jesus Christ,
that all thy children may walk in close fellow-

ship with thee; bless the Mission being undertaken in thy Name at St. ———— Church. Grant
that it may open many hearts to thy Spirit and
bring many minds to a clearer understanding of
thy truth and purpose for us; use the efforts of
our Missioner, and all who help with the Mission, for thy glory and the strengthening of the
life of thy family, the Church. Make the light
of thine Incarnate Word to shine forth in our
lives; through Jesus Christ our Lord.

### –380– *For a Mission*

Almighty God, who didst send thy Son into the
world to save sinners and to lead us into the
way of righteousness, bestow thy blessing, we
beseech thee, upon our endeavour to bring souls
to thee through this Mission and draw us ourselves to deeper consecration. May thy Holy
Spirit inspire *him* who shall speak thy word,
convince the indifferent, convert the wayward,
and in all of us renew the will to do thy will
and to continue steadfastly in thy service in the
fellowship of thy holy Church, until thy will
is done on earth as it is in heaven; through Jesus
Christ our Lord.

### –381– *Church Extension*

O Lord Jesus Christ, Who hast taught us that
it is more blessed to give than to receive, and
that to whom much is given, of them shall much

be required: pour out upon us the spirit of Thine own abundant giving; that as we have received the Churches in which we worship, we also may freely give, that others may enjoy a like inheritance, and become partakers with us in the fellowship of Thy Church; Who livest and reignest with the Father and the Holy Spirit, ever one God, world without end.

# XXIII

## CHURCH (GENERAL)

*–382– For the Church*

O God, our Father, we pray for thy Church, which is set today amid the perplexities of a changing order, and face to face with new tasks. Baptize her afresh in the life-giving spirit of Jesus. Bestow upon her a greater responsiveness to duty, a swifter compassion with suffering, and an utter loyalty to the will of God. Help her to proclaim boldly the coming of the Kingdom of God. Bid her cease from seeking her own life, lest she lose it. Make her valiant to give up her life to humanity; that, like her crucified Master, she may mount by the path of the cross to a higher glory; through the same Jesus Christ our Lord.

*–383– For the Church*

O God, of unchangeable power and eternal light, look favorably on Thy whole Church, that wonderful and sacred mystery; and by the tranquil operation of Thy perpetual Providence, carry out the work of Man's salvation; and let the whole world feel and see that things which were cast down are being raised up, and things which

had grown old are being made new, and all things are returning to perfection through Him through whom they took their origin; even through our Lord Jesus Christ.

### –384– *For the Church*

Almighty God, whose mercy is over all thy works: We praise thee for the blessings which have been brought to mankind by thy holy Church throughout all the world. We bless thee for the grace of thy Sacraments, for our fellowship in Christ with thee, and with one another; for the teaching of the Scriptures and the preaching of thy Word. We thank thee for the holy example of thy saints in all ages; for thy servants departed this life in thy faith and fear, and for the memory and example of all that has been good and true in their lives. And we humbly beseech thee that we may be numbered with them in the great company of the redeemed in heaven; through Jesus Christ our Lord.

### –385– *For the Church*

O Eternal God, who by thy Son Jesus Christ didst establish the family of thy Church in all the world, breathe upon it anew the gifts of thy Holy Spirit, that, awakening to thy command, it may go forth in lowly service, yet in conquering might, to win mankind to the love

of thy Name; through our only Saviour Jesus Christ.

## –386– *For the Church*

O Gracious Father, we humbly beseech thee for thy holy Catholic Church; that thou wouldest be pleased to fill it with all truth, in all peace. Where it is corrupt, purify it; where it is in error, direct it; where in any thing it is amiss, reform it. Where it is right, establish it; where it is in want, provide for it; where it is divided, reunite it; for the sake of him who died and rose again, and ever liveth to make intercession for us, Jesus Christ, thy Son, our Lord.

## –387– *Unity of Spirit*

O Almighty God, who hast built thy Church upon the foundation of the Apostles and Prophets, Jesus Christ himself being the head cornerstone; Grant us so to be joined together in unity of spirit by their doctrine, that we may be made an holy temple acceptable unto thee; through the same Jesus Christ our Lord.

## –388– *Power Among All Peoples*

Grant, we beseech thee, merciful God, that thy Church, being gathered together in unity by thy Holy Spirit, may manifest thy power among all peoples, to the glory of thy Name; through Jesus

Christ our Lord, who liveth and reigneth with thee and the same Spirit, one God, world without end.

### –389– *All Estates of Men*

Almighty and everlasting God, by whose Spirit the whole body of the Church is governed and sanctified; Receive our supplications and prayers, which we offer before thee for all estates of men in thy holy Church, that every member of the same, in his vocation and ministry, may truly and godly serve thee; through our Lord and Saviour Jesus Christ.

### –390– *For Those in Religious Communities*

Blessed Lord, who didst call thy disciples to follow thee in the way of sacrifice, we remember before thee those who have forsaken the natural pleasures and ambitions of life to devote themselves entirely to prayer and service of thy holy Church. In their poverty, chastity and obedience be thou their wealth, their strength and stay, that in all things they may please thee and show forth thy glory before all men.

### –391– *For Brotherhood*

O God, who showeth forth thine almighty power in mercy and compassion, and in whose love men may live together in brotherhood;

blessed is he who loveth thee, his friend in thee, and his enemy for thy sake; through Jesus Christ our Lord.

## –392– *The World-wide Church*

Eternal Father, of whom the whole family in heaven and earth is named: Unite us, as we worship Thee here, with all who in far-off places are lifting up their hands and hearts to Thee; that Thy Church throughout the world, with the Church in heaven, may offer up one sacrifice of thanksgiving; to the praise of Thy Holy Name: through Jesus Christ our Lord.

## –393– *Our Common Birthright*

O God our Father, and Father of all men, from whom all come, to whom all at last return: Bind together Thy children everywhere with the bond of mutual love, that they may claim in Thee their common birthright, and find in Thee their common service; through Jesus Christ our Lord.

# XXIV

## MISSIONS

### -394- *The Church in All the Earth*

Almighty God, whose compassions fail not, and whose loving-kindness reacheth unto the world's end; We give thee humble thanks for opening heathen lands to the light of thy truth; for making paths in the deep waters and highways in the desert; and for planting thy Church in all the earth. Grant, we beseech thee, unto us thy servants, that with lively faith we may labour abundantly to make known to all men thy blessed gift of eternal life; through Jesus Christ our Lord.

### -395- *This Thy Family*

Almighty God, we beseech thee graciously to behold this thy family, for which our Lord Jesus Christ was contented to be betrayed, and given up into the hands of wicked men, and to suffer death upon the cross; who now liveth and reigneth with thee and the Holy Ghost ever, one God, world without end.

*–396– All Who Know Thee Not*

O merciful God, who hast made all men, and
hatest nothing that thou hast made, nor desirest
the death of a sinner, but rather that he should
be converted and live; Have mercy upon all
who know thee not as thou art revealed in the
Gospel of thy Son. Take from them all ignorance, hardness of heart, and contempt of thy
Word; and so fetch them home, blessed Lord,
to thy fold, that they may be made one flock
under one shepherd, Jesus Christ our Lord, who
liveth and reigneth with thee and the Holy Spirit,
one God, world without end.

*–397– For the Heathen*

O God of all the nations of the earth: Remember the multitudes of the heathen, who, though
created in thine image, are ignorant of thy love;
and, according to the propitiation of thy Son
Jesus Christ, grant that by the prayers and labours of thy holy Church they may be delivered
from all superstition and unbelief, and brought
to worship thee; through him whom thou hast
sent to be our salvation, the Resurrection and
the Life of all the faithful, the same thy Son
Jesus Christ our Lord.

*–398– For Christian Workers*

O God our heavenly Father, we thank thee for
the gift of thy dear Son. Grant that we who
have received him in our hearts may joyfully
go forth with him on many errands. Bless those
who toil for thee in far-off places. Comfort them
in their loneliness, and unite our work to theirs.
Accept our gifts, receive our prayers, and use
us for the sake of thy Son, Jesus Christ our Lord.

*–399– For Christian Workers*

O God our Father, who didst send thy Son to
save the whole world; we pray thee to bless all
who work for thee at home and in distant lands.
Make us glad to help in thy work; so that all
thy children everywhere may learn to know thy
love, and to share with us the joy that comes
through our Saviour Jesus Christ.

*–400– For Missionaries*

O most merciful Saviour, who willest that all
men should be saved; be present with those who
are gone forth in thy Name to preach the Gospel in distant lands (*especially* ———). Be with
them in all perils, in sickness and distress, in
weariness and painfulness, in disappointment and
persecution. Give them sure confidence in thee.
Pour out upon them abundantly thy Holy Spirit,

and prosper mightily the work of their hands;
send unto them faithful and true fellow-laborers.
Give them a rich increase here, and grant that
hereafter they may dwell with thee in the heavenly places, world without end.

## –401– For Missions

O God, who hast made of one blood all the nations of men for to dwell on the face of the
whole earth; we give thee most humble and
hearty thanks for the revelation of thyself in
thy Son Jesus Christ; for the commission to thy
Church to proclaim the Gospel to every creature; for those who have gone to the ends of
the earth to bring light to them that dwell in
darkness and in the shadow of death, and for
the innumerable company who now praise thy
name out of every kindred and nation and
tongue. To thee be ascribed the praise of their
faith for ever and ever.

## –402– Medical Missions

Almighty God, Who in Thy great love towards
mankind didst send Thy Son to be the physician
both of the body and the soul; bless, we pray
Thee, the ministry of Thy missionary servants
now working in the hospitals and dispensaries of
countries overseas; and so prosper them that Thy
way may be known upon earth, Thy saving

health among all nations; through Jesus Christ
our Lord.

### -403- *For Mission Hospitals*

O Lord, the Healer of all our diseases, who
knowest how the sick have need of a physician,
let thy perpetual providence guide and direct the
work of mission hospitals throughout the world.
Instruct all whom thou hast called to be sharers
in thine own work of healing; that the pain and
grief of the world may be lightened, and the
bounds of thy Kingdom enlarged; through Jesus
Christ, our Lord.

### -404- *For Persecuted Churches and Christians*

Give salvation and strength, O King of saints,
to those who, being persecuted for righteousness'
sake, are in great tribulation; and grant that these
thy followers, loving not their lives unto the
death and leaving all to follow thee, may overcome by the word of their testimony, and over-
coming, may inherit all things.

### -405- *Our Responsibility*

O Lord, who hast warned us that thou wilt re-
quire much of those to whom much is given:
Grant that we whose lot is cast in so goodly a
heritage, may strive together the more abun-

dantly, by prayer, by almsgiving, by fasting, and by all appointed means to extend to those who know thee not what we so richly enjoy; and as we have entered into the labors of others, so to labor that others may enter into ours, to the fulfillment of thy holy will, and the salvation of all mankind; through Jesus Christ our Lord.

### –406– *The Church's Mission*

O thou Good Shepherd of the sheep, look mercifully upon those who have none to watch over them in thy Name. Prepare them to receive thy Truth, and send them pastors after thine own heart. Replenish with thine abundant grace those whom thou dost send, and awaken the pity of thy people for all who know thee not, so that by their cheerful contributions, and the cooperation of thy Holy Spirit, multitudes may be daily added to the Lord, and become partakers of the salvation which thou hast promised, O Lord and lover of souls; through Jesus Christ our Lord.

### –407– *Three Simple Prayers*

O God who hast given us the good news in thy Son Jesus Christ: So fill our hearts with thankfulness, that we may tell abroad the good tidings which we have received; through the same Jesus Christ our Lord.

O God, who hast sent thy servants to prepare thy way; fill our hearts with love and strengthen our hands to work, that we may make ready the way of our King; for Jesus Christ's sake.

Bless, O Lord, all who bear witness in thy name, by teaching, by healing, by leadership, in the far outposts of the world; and set our hearts on fire to serve thee, and to spread thy Kingdom; for Jesus Christ's sake.

*–408– Thanksgiving for Missions*

O God, mighty to save, infinite in compassion towards the nations that know thee not, and the tongues that cannot speak thy name: We humbly thank thee that thou hast made the Church of thy dear Son the chariot of the Gospel; to tell it out among the heathen that thou art King, and to bear thy love unto the world's end; and for all thy servants who counted not their lives dear unto them on this employment, and for all peoples newly praising thee, we praise and bless thee, Father, Son, and Holy Spirit, one Lord and God forever.

# XXV

## The Church in the World

### -409- *For Every Man in His Work*

Almighty God, our heavenly Father, who declarest thy glory and showest forth thy handiwork in the heavens and in the earth; Deliver us, we beseech thee, in our several callings, from the service of mammon, that we may do the work which thou givest us to do, in truth, in beauty, and in righteousness, with singleness of heart as thy servants, and to the benefit of our fellow men; for the sake of him who came among us as one that serveth, thy Son Jesus Christ our Lord.

### -410- *For Social Justice*

Almighty God, who hast created man in thine own image; Grant us grace fearlessly to contend against evil, and to make no peace with oppression; and, that we may reverently use our freedom, help us to employ it in the maintenance of justice among men and nations, to the glory of thy holy Name; through Jesus Christ our Lord.

## –411– *For All Poor, Homeless, and Neglected Folk*

O God, Almighty and merciful, who healest those that are broken in heart, and turnest the sadness of the sorrowful to joy; Let thy fatherly goodness be upon all that thou hast made. Remember in pity such as are this day destitute, homeless, or forgotten of their fellow-men. Bless the congregation of thy poor. Uplift those who are cast down. Mightily befriend innocent sufferers, and sanctify to them the endurance of their wrongs. Cheer with hope all discouraged and unhappy people, and by thy heavenly grace preserve from falling those whose penury tempteth them to sin; though they be troubled on every side, suffer them not to be distressed; though they be perplexed, save them from despair. Grant this, O Lord, for the love of him, who for our sakes became poor, thy Son, our Saviour Jesus Christ.

## –412– *A General Intercession*

O God, at whose word man goeth forth to his work and to his labour until the evening; Be merciful to all whose duties are difficult or burdensome, and comfort them concerning their toil. Shield from bodily accident and harm the workmen at their work. Protect the efforts of sober and honest industry, and suffer not the

hire of the labourers to be kept back by fraud. Incline the heart of employers and of those whom they employ to mutual forbearance, fairness, and good-will. Give the spirit of governance and of a sound mind to all in places of authority. Bless all those who labour in works of mercy or in schools of good learning. Care for all aged persons, and all little children, the sick and the afflicted, and those who travel by land or by sea. Remember all who by reason of weakness are overtasked, or because of poverty are forgotten. Let the sorrowful sighing of the prisoners come before thee; and according to the greatness of thy power, preserve thou those that are appointed to die. Give ear unto our prayer, O merciful and gracious Father, for the love of thy dear Son, our Saviour Jesus Christ.

### –413– *For Those Engaged in Industry*

O God, the father of all mankind, we beseech thee to inspire us with such love, truth, and equity, that in all our dealings one with another we may show forth our brotherhood in thee; for the sake of Jesus Christ our Lord.

### –414– *For Those Engaged in Industry*

O God, who hast taught us that we are members one of another, remove, we beseech thee, from among us all distrust and bitterness in industrial disputes; and grant that, seeking what is just and

equal, and caring for the needs of others, we may live and work together in unity and love; through Jesus Christ our Lord.

## –415– *For Goodwill in Industry*

Father of all, who didst send thine only Son to bring peace on earth, goodwill towards men; fulfil the purpose of his coming by increasing goodwill and preserving peace between employers and employed. To all who lead in industry and labor give the desire to seek not power and privilege for themselves but the common good of all, and by justice, mutual consideration, and faithful work, advance our national well-being.

## –416– *Labor and Industry*

O God, who in thy providence hast appointed to every man his work: we humbly beseech thee to put away all strife and contention, between those who are engaged in the labors of industry and those who employ their labor. Deliver them from all greed and covetousness, and grant that they, seeking only that which is just and equal, may live and work together in brotherly union and concord, to thy glory, their own well-being, and the prosperity of their country; through Jesus Christ our Lord.

*-417- For Equal Opportunities*

O God, we beseech thee, give us that world in
which it shall be accounted shame and mean-
ness for employers to tyrannize and for workmen
to shirk, in which men's consciences will not
permit people in any land to starve or the few
to enjoy leisure at the expense of the many, and
in which all children shall have the right to the
same opportunities for education. If the way to
this order shall lie through pain and sorrow
and struggle, give us the patience and the fortitude to bear it in view of the brighter day to
come. And in thy good time transform that better order into the Kingdom of thy love; through
Jesus Christ our Lord.

*-418- Righteous Discontent*

O God, who hast taught us the joy of serving
thee and hast given us an earnest of the peace
that passeth understanding, fill us also with
righteous discontent, that we may never be per-
fectly at rest while injustice is done to thy people and thy children cry out in anguish; grant
us so to desire thy Kingdom, as a pearl of great
price, that the signs of its coming may be seen
upon earth; through Jesus Christ our Lord.

### –419– *The Kingdom*

O God, whose Kingdom is everlasting and power infinite, and whose glory the heaven of heavens cannot contain, grant us so to desire thy Kingdom, as a pearl of great price, that the signs of its coming may be seen among men; through Jesus Christ our Lord.

### –420– *Through Things Common*

O Master of the hearts of men, make us ill content with any peace save that of our Saviour, who won his peace after he had made the world's ills his own. Hold us back when, in our vulgarity, we would go apart from the path and life of the lowly. As our Saviour made the carpenter's shop his school and from it passed to the perfection of Calvary, so may we keep ourselves close to the lives of the great body of men, and pass through things common into the things eternal; through Jesus Christ our Saviour.

### –421– *The Unemployed*

O Lord and heavenly Father, we commend to Thy care and protection the men and women of this land who are suffering distress and anxiety through lack of work. Strengthen and support them, we beseech Thee; and so prosper the counsels of those who govern and direct our indus-

tries, that Thy people may be set free from want and fear to work in peace and security, for the relief of their necessities and the well-being of this realm; through Jesus Christ our Lord.

### —422— Fellow-Workers

O God, who hast bound us together in this bundle of life, give us grace to understand how our lives depend upon the courage, the industry, the honesty, and the integrity of our fellow-men; that we may be mindful of their needs, grateful for their faithfulness, and faithful in our responsibilities to them; through Jesus Christ our Lord.

### —423— The City

Grant us, O Lord, a vision of this city, fair as it might be in fulfilment of Thy purpose: a city of justice, where none shall prey upon others; a city of plenty, where greed and poverty shall be done away; a city of brotherhood, where success is founded upon service, and honour is given to nobleness alone; a city of peace, where order shall not rest on force, but on love of all for each and each for all. Hear Thou, O Lord, our prayer and pledge of love and service; and hasten the day of the eternal city which cometh down from heaven to earth from Thee, through Jesus Christ our Lord.

### –424– *For All Who Influence Public Opinion*

Almighty God, who hast proclaimed thine eternal truth by the voice of prophets and evangelists: Direct and bless, we beseech thee, those who in this our generation speak where many listen and write what many read; that they may do their part in making the heart of the people wise, its mind sound, and its will righteous; to the honor of Jesus Christ our Lord.

### –425– *For Communication of the Gospel*

O Almighty God, we thank thee for the wonderful universe thou hast created and for its secrets revealed to men. We thank thee that men may speak to one another across the centuries and across the continents, annihilating space and time. Grant that all means of communication may be used for the purpose of truth, peace, and love, so that all men may hear the good news of the gospel and find their brotherhood in thee; through Jesus Christ, thine own Eternal Word.

### –426– *The World Family*

O God, the creator of the ends of the earth, with whom there is no distinction of race or habitation, but all are one in Thee: Break down, we beseech Thee, the barriers which divide us; that we may work together in one accord with each

other and with Thee; through Him who is the Saviour of all, Jesus Christ Thy Son our Lord.

### -427- *Workers with Mind and Hand*

O blessed Saviour, Who wast pleased Thyself to be numbered among the craftsmen: we pray Thee to guide and prosper all who labor with mind and hand, that their work may be done for Thy honor and rewarded with Thine approval Who livest and reignest with the Father and the Holy Spirit, one God, world without end.

### -428- *For Leaders*

O God, Almighty Father, King of kings and Lord of all our rulers, grant that the hearts and minds of all who go out as leaders before us, the statesmen, the judges, the men of learning and the men of wealth, may be so filled with the love of thy laws and of that which is righteous and life-giving, that they may serve as a wholesome salt unto the earth, and be worthy stewards of thy good and perfect gifts, through Jesus Christ our Lord.

### -429- *For Magistrates*

O heavenly Father, at whose hand the weak shall take no wrong nor the mighty escape just judgment; pour thy grace upon thy servants our judges and magistrates, that by their true, fruit-

ful and diligent execution of justice to all men
equally, thou mayest be glorified, the common
wealth daily promoted, and we all live in peace
and quietness, godliness and virtue; through Jesus
Christ our Lord.

## –430– *For Justice*

O God, the King of righteousness, lead us, we
pray thee, in the ways of justice and of peace;
inspire us to break down all oppression and
wrong, to gain for every man his due reward,
and from every man his due service; that each
may live for all, and all may care for each, in
the name of Jesus Christ our Lord.

## –431– *Workers on the Land*

Almighty God, who hast blessed the earth that
it should be fruitful and bring forth abundantly
whatsoever is needful for the life of man, prosper,
we beseech thee, the labours of those who work
on the land and grant such seasonable weather
that we may gather the fruits of the earth and
proclaim thy great goodness with thanksgiving;
through Jesus Christ our Lord.

## –432– *Workers in the City*

O God, whose Son Jesus Christ wrought as a
craftsman amongst the sons of men, we ask thy
blessing on all the toiling thousands of our cities.

Grant to those who employ them a sense of justice and sympathy, and to those who labour a knowledge of the dignity and worth of their work. Keep us from prejudice of class or education, and help us to bring about a brotherhood of men, so that all may work gladly to build a city where slums are no more, oppression has ceased, competition is fair, and thou mayest be ever glorified in praise and worship and work; through Jesus Christ our Lord.

## -433- *For Those Who Work in Offices*

O God, graciously grant us strength and wisdom in the doing of our various tasks and thy guiding hand in all the scattered details that make up our lives; renew in us daily a sense of joy and grant, we beseech thee, that in this busy world we may help those whose lives touch ours to know and love thee; through Jesus Christ our Lord.

## -434- *For the Whole Human Family*

Almighty God, look as a Father upon all nations and kindreds and people and tongues, and let the barriers which separate thy children be broken down that we may grow in concord.

Grant to us, O God, a right regard for the differences in individuals and groups and races, and an understanding of the ministries of difference

in thy manifold design for life; imbue us with the charity which makes the alienating fact of no effect and by which the far becomes the near; and by the tranquil operation of thy Holy Spirit moving in the minds of men, diminish our dissensions and divisions, that peace with righteousness may be increased within thy human family; through Jesus Christ our Lord.

## -435- For All Who Do Good in the World

Almighty God, look with favor upon those whose lives add to the world's good: who are humble in self-estimate, averse to self-seeking, ready for self-sacrifice: who are upright and trustworthy, kindly and generous, discerning and compassionate: who do not despise others nor take advantage of them nor contrive against them nor condemn them with arrogance, but communicate blessing.

Reward them, O God, for their goodness; let it evoke gratitude and induce imitation; let it not be obscured or nullified by their intermittent failures; and grant to them, thy faithful servants, the benediction of thy sure support; through Jesus Christ our Lord.

## -436- For All Who Do Evil in the World

Almighty God, look in mercy upon those whose sins afflict the world with evil: whose self-will or pride of life, whose greed for gain or place or

pleasure or dominion, whose malice or injustice,
whose callousness or cruelty, work hurt and harm
and havoc on the earth.

Dispose and enable them, O God, to follow the
sense of right which they may cherish secretly;
set straight in them the thoughts and the desires
which have been twisted by misfortune or bad
environment and influence; grant that their evil
may be overcome with good; and help society
to remedy the wrongs which breed corruption,
that wholesome brotherhood may win its way
among us; through Jesus Christ our Lord.

### –437– *For All Who Are Without Faith*

Almighty God, look upon those who have not
come to know thee or who do not acknowledge
thee: on those who are confused in mind and
doubt thee because of life's bewilderments and
riddles, or who do not think of thee or turn to
thee because of its entanglements and pressures:
and on those who even while professing faith
yet live without it.

Speak to them, O God, by whatever voices they
can hear and heed; let them be enlightened by
the witness of all who herald and exemplify thy
truth; let them be upheld by the prayers of all
who pray believing; and bring them to the haven
where unknowing they would be; through Jesus
Christ our Lord.

# XXVI

## Ecumenical

### -438- *For Church Unity*

O God, in whose One Gospel all men are made One; let not thy saving work fail in the broken order of Christendom because we have failed to understand thy message. Prosper the labors of all churches bearing the name of Christ and striving to further righteousness and faith in him. Help us to place the truth above our conception of it, and joyfully to recognize the presence of the Holy Spirit wherever he may choose to dwell among men; through Jesus Christ our Lord.

### -439- *For Church Unity*

O God our Heavenly Father, whose blessed Son came to bring mankind into one family in thee; we pray for the unity of the Church in all the world. As we became divided through what was believed to be our loyalty to our Lord, so by our loyalty to him now help us to seek to heal the divisions which keep us from one another and weaken our efforts to extend thy kingdom in the earth. Give us understanding of other people's points of view; save us from prejudice; and grant that as we see clearly our Saviour's

will that His Church may be one, so we may labor in love to bring it to pass; through Jesus Christ our Lord.

## -440- For Church Unity

O Almighty God, who hast built thy Church upon the foundation of the Apostles and Prophets, Jesus Christ himself being the chief Corner-Stone; grant that, by the operation of thy Spirit, all Christians may be so joined together in unity of spirit, and in the bond of peace, that they may be an holy temple acceptable unto thee; through the same thy Son Jesus Christ our Lord.

## -441- For Christian Unity

O God of Peace, who through thy Son Jesus Christ didst set forth one Faith for the salvation of mankind; Send thy grace and heavenly blessing upon all Christian people who are striving to draw nearer to thee, and to each other, in the unity of the Spirit and in the bond of peace. Give us penitence for our divisions, wisdom to know thy truth, courage to do thy will, love which shall break down the barriers of pride and prejudice, and an unswerving loyalty to thy holy Name. Suffer us not to shrink from any endeavor, which is in accordance with thy will, for the peace and unity of thy Church. Give us boldness to seek only thy glory and the advancement of thy Kingdom. Unite us all in thee as

thou, O Father, with thy Son and the Holy
Spirit, art one God, world without end.

### -442- For Christian Unity

O Lord Jesus Christ, who didst pray for thy
disciples that they might be one even as thou
art one with the Father; draw us to thyself, that,
in common love and obedience to thee, we may
be united to one another in the fellowship of the
one Spirit, that the world may believe that thou
art Lord, to the glory of God the Father.

### -443- For Christian Unity

O God, our Father, of whom every family in
heaven and earth is named: So strengthen us
with might by thy Spirit, that, knowing the love
of Christ in our hearts, we may patiently establish that holy fellowship which is the mystical
body of the Prince of Peace; through the same
thy son Jesus Christ our Lord.

### -444- For the Unity of God's People

O God, the Father of our Lord Jesus Christ, our
only Saviour, the Prince of Peace; Give us grace
seriously to lay to heart the great dangers we
are in by our unhappy divisions. Take away all
hatred and prejudice, and whatsoever else may
hinder us from godly union and concord: that
as there is but one Body and one Spirit, and one

hope of our calling, one Lord, one Faith, one Baptism, one God and Father of us all, so we may be all of one heart and of one soul, united in one holy bond of truth and peace, of faith and charity, and may with one mind and one mouth glorify thee; through Jesus Christ our Lord.

## –445– *A Prayer for the Universal Church*

O God, of whom every fatherhood in heaven and on earth is named, in whose earthly family there is neither Jew nor Greek, male nor female, bond nor free, but only children standing in equal need and equally sharing thy fatherly care; Grant that thy Church, being quickened by thy love, may manifest to the world the unity to which thou hast called it in the gospel of thy Son, and by the fellowship of his disciples bring healing to the world.

## –446– *Christlike Charity*

O Lord Jesus Christ, who art the Door by whom, if any man enter in, he shall be saved: Open unto us who knock, that, evermore abiding within the ample household of thy redeeming charity, we may live as true brothers of all whom thou dost love; for thy Name's sake.

### -447- *The Church*

God, our Shepherd, give to the Church a new vision and a new charity, new wisdom and fresh understanding, the revival of her brightness and the renewal of her unity; that the eternal message of Thy Son, undefiled by the traditions of men, may be hailed as the good news of the new age; through Him Who maketh all things new, Jesus Christ our Lord.

### -448- *The Church Under Persecution*

Be merciful, O Father of all mercies, to thy Church universal dispersed throughout the whole world; and grant that all they that confess thy holy name may agree in the truth of thy holy word, and live in godly concord and unity. And especially be merciful to such as are under persecution for the testimony of their conscience, and profession of the gospel of thy Son our Saviour Jesus Christ.

### -449- *The Broken Body*

Eternal God, look mercifully upon the broken body of thy Church. Draw its members unto thee and one to another by the bands of thy love; that its restored unity may bring healing to the nations, and the life of mankind may glorify thee; through Jesus Christ our Lord.

# XXVII

## Thanksgiving

### -450- *A General Thanksgiving*

Almighty God, Father of all mercies, we, thine unworthy servants, do give thee most humble and hearty thanks for all thy goodness and loving-kindness to us, and to all men. We bless thee for our creation, preservation, and all the blessings of this life; but above all, for thine inestimable love in the redemption of the world by our Lord Jesus Christ; for the means of grace, and for the hope of glory. And, we beseech thee, give us that due sense of all thy mercies, that our hearts may be unfeignedly thankful; and that we show forth thy praise, not only with our lips, but in our lives, by giving up our selves to thy service, and by walking before thee in holiness and righteousness all our days; through Jesus Christ our Lord, to whom, with thee and the Holy Ghost, be all honour and glory, world without end.

### -451- *A Thanksgiving*

Almighty God, Father of all mercies, we thank thee for all thou hast given and for all thou hast forgiven; for thy hidden blessings and for those

which in our negligence we have passed over: for
every gift of nature or of grace: for our power
of loving: for all which thou hast yet in store for
us: for everything, whether joy or sorrow,
whereby thou art drawing us to thyself through
Jesus Christ our Lord.

## *–452– A Thanksgiving*

O Thou, Who art the hope of all the ends of the
earth, and on Whom the eyes of all do wait,
Who crownest the year with Thy goodness, and
openest Thine hand and fillest all things living
with plenteousness: every day we give thanks
unto Thee, and praise Thy Name for ever and
ever; through Jesus Christ our Lord.

## *–453– A Thanksgiving*

Accept, O Lord God, our Father, the sacrifices
of our thanksgiving; this, of praise, for Thy
great mercies already afforded to us; and this,
of prayer, for the continuance and enlargement
of them; this, of penitence, for such only recom-
pense as our sinful nature can endeavor; and this,
of the love of our hearts, as the only gift Thou
dost ask or desire; and all these, through the all-
holy and atoning sacrifice of Jesus Christ Thy
Son our Saviour.

*-454- A Thanksgiving*

Help us to pray always and not to faint, in everything giving thanks, offering up the sacrifice of praise continually, possessing our souls in patience, and learning in whatsoever state we are therewith to be content; for the sake of Jesus Christ our Lord and Master.

*-455- A Thanksgiving*

O Lord God, our Heavenly Father, we thank Thee that Thou hast called us to the knowledge of Thy grace, and faith in Thee. Increase this knowledge, and confirm this faith in us evermore. We thank Thee for all those who are called by Thy name in all parts of the world, praying Thee that they may steadfastly walk in the way that leadeth to eternal life. We thank Thee for all Thy servants departed this life in Thy faith and fear, beseeching Thee to give us grace so to follow their good examples, that with them we may be made partakers of Thy heavenly kingdom. Grant this, O Father, for Jesus Christ's sake, our only Mediator and Advocate.

*-456- A Thanksgiving*

For the benison of sunshine, and the beauty of
    rain;
For birdsong at morning and starshine at night;

For good and many-tasting food, for the great
    gift of sleep;
For the discoveries of science, and the heritage
    of art;
For the ministry of books, and for music, beyond
    the reach of words;
For the care of fathers and mothers, and the
    happiness of home;
For the sanity of friendship, and the madness of
    love,
Thanks be to the Lord, our God.

### –457– *A Thanksgiving for the Fruits of the Earth*

Most gracious God, by whose knowledge the
depths are broken up, and the clouds drop down
the dew; We yield thee unfeigned thanks and
praise for the return of seed-time and harvest,
for the increase of the ground and the gathering
in of the fruits thereof, and for all the other
blessings of thy merciful providence bestowed
upon this nation and people. And, we beseech
thee, give us a just sense of these great mercies;
such as may appear in our lives by an humble,
holy, and obedient walking before thee all our
days; through Jesus Christ our Lord, to whom,
with thee and the Holy Ghost, be all glory and
honour, world without end.

## *-458-* For Thanksgiving Day

Almighty God, we thank thee for all the blessings of this life, and today especially for those that are ours in this free land; for the fruits of the soil, the untold resources of the earth, the opportunities for work and play and healthful living; for liberty in speech and written word; for public education and regard for every man's welfare. And we pray thee that, as we thank thee for these and all thy mercies, thou wilt continue thy good hand upon us and make our nation great in that greatness which alone is pleasing to thee, even the righteousness that is the doing of thy holy will.

## *-459-* Seedtime and Harvest

O Almighty God, Who in Thine unfailing providence givest food to all flesh: vouchsafe, we beseech Thee, to bless the seed sown in our fields, and to grant that, having received Thy good gifts in due season, we may ever with thankful hearts offer up our praises unto Thee; through Jesus Christ our Lord.

## *-460-* Seedtime and Harvest

O Gracious Father, Who openest Thine hands and fillest all things living with plenteousness: vouchsafe to bless the lands and multiply the har-

vest of the world; let Thy breath go forth to
renew the face of the earth; show Thy loving-
kindness, that our land may give her increase;
and so fill us with good things that the poor and
needy may give thanks unto Thy Name through
Jesus Christ our Lord.

## –461– Seedtime and Harvest

Almighty God, Who crownest the year with
Thy goodness, we beseech Thee to bless with
Thy bounty the farmers and workers on the
land, that as they sow in hope so in due time
they may gather in the sheaves with joy; through
Jesus Christ our Lord.

## –462– In Time of Scarcity

O God, our heavenly Father, who by thy blessed
Son hast taught us to ask our daily bread of thee;
behold, we beseech thee, the afflictions of thy
people, and send us a seasonable relief in this
our necessity. Increase the fruits of the earth
by thy heavenly benediction, and grant that we,
receiving with thankfulness thy gracious gifts,
may use the same to thy glory, the relief of those
that are needy, and our own comfort; through
Jesus Christ our Lord.

## -463- *For God Revealed in Saintly Lives*

Holy Father, we thank thee for the light of the Gospel shining in our world. We thank thee for all who have walked therein, and especially for those so dear to us, in whose lives we have seen thy glory and beauty. May we know that whether in the body or out of the body they are with thee, and that when these earthly days are come to an end, it is not that our service of thee and of one another may cease, but that it may begin anew; through Him who is the Light of the World, thy Son, our Lord.

## -464- *For God's Best Gifts*

O God of Love, we yield thee thanks for whatsoever thou hast given us richly to enjoy, for health and vigor, for the love and care of home, for joys of friendship, and for every good gift of happiness and strength. We praise thee for all thy servants who by their example and encouragement have helped us on our way, and for every vision of thyself which thou hast ever given us in sacrament or prayer; and we humbly beseech thee that all these thy benefits we may use in thy service and to the glory of thy Holy Name; through Jesus Christ, thy Son, our Lord.

### -465- *For Joy in God's Creation*

O heavenly Father, who hast filled the world with beauty; Open, we beseech thee, our eyes to behold thy gracious hand in all thy works; that rejoicing in thy whole creation, we may learn to serve thee with gladness, for the sake of him by whom all things were made, thy Son, Jesus Christ our Lord.

### -466- *For Saints in Common Life*

We thank Thee, O Lord, for all who have chosen poverty or solitude for Thy sake, for men of prayer, for saints in common life who have borne suffering for noble ends, and for those who have endured pain with patience and purity of life, in the strength of Him Who for the joy that was set before Him endured the Cross, even Jesus Christ our Lord.

### -467- *Thanksgiving for God's Gifts*

O Thou light of my heart, Thou bread of my inmost soul, thanks be to Thee, my joy and my glory, my confidence and my God, thanks be to Thee for Thy gifts. Preserve them to me, for so wilt Thou preserve me myself, and those things shall be enlarged and perfected which Thou hast given me, and I myself shall be with Thee, Who didst give me being ———— O Lord, my God, I lay my whole heart upon the altar of Thy

praise, a whole burnt-offering of praise I offer
to Thee. Let the flame of Thy love set afire my
whole heart; let nothing in me be left to myself,
nothing wherein to look to myself; but may I
burn wholly before Thee. Lord, let Thy fire con-
sume all that is mine: let all be Thine.

## –468– *Praise and Thanksgiving*

O Lord our God, Who hast bidden the light to
shine out of darkness, Who hast again wakened
us to praise Thy goodness and ask for Thy
grace; accept now, in Thy endless mercy, the
sacrifice of our worship and thanksgiving, and
grant unto us all such requests as may be wholesome for us. Make us to be children of the light
and of the day, and heirs of Thy everlasting inheritance. Remember, O Lord, according to the
multitude of Thy mercies, Thy whole Church;
all who join with us in prayer, all our brethren
by land or sea, or wherever they may be in Thy
vast kingdom who stand in need of Thy grace
and succour. Pour out upon them the riches of
Thy mercy, so that we, redeemed in soul and
body, and steadfast in faith, may ever praise Thy
wonderful and holy Name; through Jesus Christ
our Lord.

## –469– *For Christian Witness*

All glory, thanks, and praise be to Thee, O Lord
our God and Saviour, for those who take up

their cross and follow bravely after Thee. For those who tread the way of sorrow in the calm of faith. For those who battle for the right, in Thy strength. For those who bear physical pain with sweet and sanctifying grace. For those who endure petty slights forgivingly. For those who rise above still greater wrongs. For those who continue their duties conscientiously whether so recognized or not. For those, who by Thy heavenly wisdom are enabled to teach the way of life. For those who tend Thy flock with diligent care. For those who love others unselfishly in Thee. All glory be to Thee, O Lord most high.

### –470– *For Great and Simple Joys*

Let us praise and thank God for all great and simple joys;

For the gift of wonder and the joy of discovery; for the everlasting freshness of experience;

For all that comes to us through sympathy and through sorrow, and for the joy of work attempted and achieved;

For musicians, poets and craftsmen, and for all who work in form and color to increase the beauty of life;

For the likeness of Christ in ordinary people, their forbearance, courage and kindness, and for all obscure and humble lives of service;

Glory be to the Father and to the Son and to the Holy Ghost ever world without end.

# XXVIII

## Seasons and Days

*–471– Advent*

Almighty God, give us grace that we may cast away the works of darkness, and put upon us the armour of light, now in the time of this mortal life, in which thy Son Jesus Christ came to visit us in great humility; that in the last day, when he shall come again in his glorious majesty to judge both the quick and the dead, we may rise to the life immortal, through him who liveth and reigneth with thee and the Holy Ghost, now and ever.

*–472– Advent*

Almighty Father, Whose blessed Son at His coming amongst us brought redemption unto His people and peace to men of goodwill: grant that, when He shall come again in glory to judge the world and to make all things new, we may be found ready to receive Him, and enter into His joy; through the same our Lord Jesus Christ.

### –473– *Advent*

O God, Who didst look on man when he had fallen down into death, and resolve to redeem him by the advent of Thine only begotten Son; grant, we beseech Thee, that they who confess His glorious Incarnation may also be admitted to the fellowship of Him their Redeemer; through the same Jesus Christ our Lord.

### –474– *Advent*

O Lord, raise up, we pray thee, thy power, and come among us, and with great might succour us; that whereas, through our sins and wickedness, we are sore let and hindered in running the race that is set before us, thy bountiful grace and mercy may speedily help and deliver us; through Jesus Christ our Lord, to whom, with thee and the Holy Ghost, be honour and glory, world without end.

### –475– *Christmas Eve*

We commit unto thee, O God, in this silent hour, all our Christmas plans, our hopes, our daily work, our families and family reunions, our gaieties and our griefs—asking thy blessing upon every thought and endeavor, thy control over every enterprise, thy Spirit of charity in our hearts and wisdom in our minds; that when thy

Son our Lord cometh he may find in us a mansion prepared for himself; through the same, our Saviour Jesus Christ.

### –476– *Christmas Eve*

Send, O God, into the darkness of this troubled world, the light of the Son: Let the star of thy hope touch the minds of all men with the bright beams of mercy and truth; and so direct our steps that we may ever walk in the way revealed to us, as the shepherds of Bethlehem walked with joy to the manger where he dwelt who now and ever reigns in our hearts, Jesus Christ our Lord.

### –477– *Christmas*

O God, of heavenly glory, Source of earthly peace and good will: May our Christmas be merry because touched with joy divine; through him who in his purity and love is born in our hearts today, thy Son, Jesus Christ our Lord.

### –478– *Christmas*

O Son of God, who from the beginning wast with the Father, and who for us men and for our salvation came down from heaven; Grant us more and more to receive of thy fulness, and to accept of thee the power to become the sons of God; for thy sake who art the true light of every

man that cometh into the world, now and for
ever.

## –479– *Christmas*

O heavenly Father, who hast declared thy love
to men by the birth of the Holy Child at Bethlehem, help us to welcome him with gladness and
to make room for him in our common days; so
that we may live at peace with one another,
and in good will with all thy family; through the
same thy Son Jesus Christ our Lord.

## –480– *Christmas*

O Blessed Lord Jesus, give us thankful hearts
today for Thee, our choicest gift, our dearest
guest. Let not our souls be busy inns that have
no room for Thee and Thine, but quiet homes of
prayer and praise where Thou mayest find fit
company, where the needful cares of life are
wisely ordered and put away, and wide, sweet
spaces kept for Thee, where holy thoughts pass
up and down, and fervent longings watch for
and wait Thy coming. So, when Thou comest
again, O Blessed One, mayest Thou find all
things ready, and Thy servants waiting for no
new master, but for one long loved and known.
Even so, come, Lord Jesus.

*–481– Christmas*

O God, Whose blessed Son Jesus Christ became man that we might become the sons of God: grant, we beseech Thee, that being made partakers of the divine nature of Thy Son, we may be conformed to His likeness; Who liveth and reigneth with Thee and the Holy Ghost, now and ever.

*–482– Christmas*

Almighty God, who hast poured upon us the new light of thine incarnate Word; Grant that the same light enkindled in our hearts may shine forth in our lives; through Jesus Christ our Lord.

*–483– Christmas*

O Almighty God, Who by the Birth of Thy holy Child Jesus hast given us a great Light to dawn upon our darkness, grant, we pray Thee, that in His light we may see light to the end of our days; and bestow upon us, we beseech Thee, that most excellent Christmas gift of charity to all men, that so, the likeness of Thy Son may be formed in us, and that we may have the ever-brightening hope of everlasting life; through Jesus Christ our Lord.

### –484– Christmas

O God, who when the fullness of the time was come didst send forth Thy Son, born of a woman, to redeem mankind; Hasten the day of His dominion in all lands, and the increase of His government and of peace; to whom, with Thee and the Holy Ghost, be all honor and glory, world without end.

### –485– Christmas

O Blessed Jesus, Saviour of mankind, at whose birth the night was filled with heavenly radiance: Lighten the thick darkness of the world, and the gloom of our miseries and fears; Have compassion upon the peoples of the earth stumbling in confusion, and guide their feet into the way of peace: Who art with the Father and the Holy Ghost one God, world without end.

### –486– Christmas

O Lord Jesus Christ, who took upon Thee to deliver man, and in whom alone is the world's salvation: Mercifully behold the earth in disquietude and the peoples in perplexity and fear; Rise, O Thou Sun of Righteousness, with healing in Thy beams, and grant us deliverance and peace; who art with the Father and the Holy Ghost, God blessed forever.

*–487– Christmas*

O Gracious Father, who sent not Thy Son into the world to condemn the world, but that the world through Him might be saved: Fulfil the good tidings of Thine Angel, and bring great joy to all people through His Nativity who is the Prince of Peace: To whom, with Thee and the Holy Ghost, be glory in the highest, now and forevermore.

*–488– Epiphany*

We thank Thee O God, that Thou didst give Thy Son Jesus Christ to be the light of the world, and that in Him Thou hast revealed Thy glory and the wonder of Thy saving love. Help us to love Thee who hast so loved us; strengthen us for the service of Thy kingdom; and grant that the light of Christ may so shine throughout the world that men everywhere may be drawn to Him who is the Saviour and Lord of all, and the whole earth be filled with Thy glory, through Jesus Christ, our Lord.

*–489– Epiphany*

O God, Who didst manifest Thy only begotten Son to the Gentiles, and hast commanded Thy Church to preach the Gospel to every creature, bless all Thy servants who are labouring for

Thee in distant lands. Have compassion upon the heathen and upon all who know Thee not. Lead them by Thy Holy Spirit to Him Who is the Light of the World, that walking in the light they may at length attain to the light of everlasting life; through Jesus Christ our Lord.

### –490– *Epiphany*

Almighty and everlasting God, the brightness of faithful souls, Who didst bring the Gentiles to Thy light, and made known unto them Him Who is the true Light and the bright and morning Star, fill we beseech Thee, the world with Thy glory, and show Thyself by the radiance of Thy Light unto all nations; through Jesus Christ our Lord.

### –491– *Lent*

Almighty God, whose most dear Son went not up to joy but first he suffered pain, and entered not into glory before he was crucified; Mercifully grant that we, walking in the way of the cross, may find it none other than the way of life and peace; through the same thy Son Jesus Christ our Lord.

### –492– *Lent*

O God, who by Thy care and counsel for mankind hast moved Thy Church to appoint this

holy season wherein the hearts of those who seek
Thee may receive Thy help and healing: we beseech Thee, Saviour of our souls and bodies, to
purify us by Thy discipline, that, abiding in
Thee and Thou in us, we may grow in grace
and in the faith and knowledge of Thee; through
Jesus Christ our Lord.

### *-493- Ash Wednesday*

O God, who by Thy Word dost marvelously
work out the reconciliation of mankind; grant,
we beseech Thee, that by this holy fast we may
both be subjected to Thee with all our hearts,
and be united to each other in prayer to Thee;
through Jesus Christ our Lord.

### *-494- Ash Wednesday*

Almighty and everlasting God, who hatest nothing that thou hast made, and dost forgive the
sins of all those who are penitent; Create and
make in us new and contrite hearts, that we,
worthily lamenting our sins and acknowledging
our wretchedness, may obtain of thee, the God
of all mercy, perfect remission and forgiveness;
through Jesus Christ our Lord.

### *-495- Ash Wednesday*

Give me grace, O my Father, to be utterly
ashamed of my own reluctance. Rouse me from

sloth and coldness, and make me desire Thee with my whole heart. Teach me to love meditation, sacred reading, and prayer. Teach me to love that which must engage my mind for all eternity.

## –496– Ash Wednesday

O Father of mercies and God of all comforts, Who by Thy Blessed Son hast declared, that all sins shall be forgiven unto the sons of men upon their true repentance, let this most comfortable word support us Thy servants against the temptations of the devil. Though our sins are great, they cannot be too great for Thy mercy, which is infinite. O give us true repentance for all the errors of our life past, and steadfast faith in Thy Son Jesus Christ, that our sins may be done away by Thy mercy; through the merits of the same Jesus Christ our Lord.

## –497– Holy Week

Assist us mercifully with thy help, O Lord God of our salvation; that we may enter with joy upon the meditation of those mighty acts, whereby thou hast given unto us life and immortality; through Jesus Christ our Lord.

## –498– Palm Sunday

As on this day we keep the special memory of our Redeemer's entry into the city, so grant, O

Lord, that now and ever He may triumph in our hearts. Let the King of grace and glory enter in, and let us lay ourselves and all we are in full and joyful homage before Him; through the same Jesus Christ our Lord.

## –499– *Palm Sunday*

Almighty and everlasting God, who, of thy tender love towards mankind, hast sent thy Son, our Saviour Jesus Christ, to take upon him our flesh, and to suffer death upon the cross, that all mankind should follow the example of his great humility; Mercifully grant, that we may both follow the example of his patience, and also be made partakers of his resurrection; through the same Jesus Christ our Lord.

## –500– *Maundy Thursday*

Almighty Father, whose dear Son, on the night before he suffered, did institute the Sacrament of his Body and Blood; Mercifully grant that we may thankfully receive the same in remembrance of him, who in these holy mysteries giveth us a pledge of life eternal; the same thy Son Jesus Christ our Lord, who now liveth and reigneth with thee and the Holy Spirit ever, one God, world without end.

### –501– Maundy Thursday

Lord Jesus Christ, Who when Thou wast able
to institute Thy Holy Sacrament at the Last
Supper, didst wash the feet of the Apostles, and
teach us by Thy example the grace of humility:
cleanse us, we beseech Thee, from all stain of
sin, that we may be worthy partakers of Thy
holy mysteries; Who livest and reignest with the
Father and the Holy Ghost, one God, world
without end.

### –502– Good Friday

O Christ, our God, Who for us sinners didst
endure the Cross and so didst enlighten the
world's darkness: visit our hearts, we beseech
Thee, with Thy heavenly light, and open the
eyes of our minds to know Thee as Thou art,
Thou lover of souls; Who through death didst
destroy death and ever livest to make intercession for us; and with the Father and the Holy
Spirit art one God, for ever and ever.

### –503– Good Friday

Lord Jesus, we beseech Thee, by the loneliness of
Thy suffering on the cross, be near unto all
them that are desolate, in pain, or in sorrow. Let
Thy presence sustain them, and, by Thy loving

power, heal and console them according to their need.

### –504– Good Friday

O Thou Prince of Peace, Who, when Thou wast reviled, reviledst not again, and on the cross didst pray for Thy murderers, implant in our hearts the virtues of gentleness and patience, that we may overcome evil with good, for Thy sake love our enemies, and as children of our heavenly Father seek Thy peace, and evermore rejoice in Thy love; through Jesus Christ our Saviour.

### –505– Good Friday

Almighty God, who hast shown us the true way of blessedness in the life and teaching of Thy Son and in His suffering and death dost teach us that the path of love may lead to the Cross, and that the reward of faithfulness may be a crown of thorns; Give us grace to learn these hard lessons, and to take up our Cross and follow Christ in the strength of patience, and in the constancy of faith. And may we have such fellowship with Him in His sorrow, that we may know the secret of His strength and peace, and even in our darkest hour of trial and anguish see the shining of the eternal light; through the same Jesus Christ our Lord.

### -506- *Good Friday*

Saviour, who in human flesh didst conquer tears
by crying, pain by suffering, death by dying,
we, thy servants gather before the Cross to com-
memorate thy passion and to contemplate anew
the wonder of thy compassionate love. As we
listen to thy gracious words uttered with dying
lips, illumine our souls that we may know the
truth, melt our hearts that we may hate our sins,
nerve our wills that we may do thy bidding; to
the glory of thy name and our own eternal gain.

### -507- *Easter*

O God, who for our redemption didst give thine
only-begotten Son to the death of the Cross,
and by his glorious resurrection hast delivered us
from the power of our enemy; Grant us so to
die daily from sin, that we may evermore live
with him in the joy of his resurrection; through
the same thy Son Christ our Lord.

### -508- *Easter*

O gracious Lord, Who as at this time, didst raise
Thy Son Jesus Christ with power from the grave,
raise us up, we beseech Thee, from the death of
sin to the life of righteousness; Revive our faith,
and make us followers of Him Who hath taken
away the "sin of the world; Who by His death
hath destroyed death, and by His rising to life

again hath restored to us everlasting life." Hear
us, O merciful Father, we pray Thee, for the
sake of our risen Saviour, to Whom, with Thee
and the Holy Ghost, be all honour and glory,
world without end.

### –509– *Easter*

O God, who through thine only begotten Son
Jesus Christ hast overcome death and opened
unto us the gate of everlasting life; grant that,
as he was raised from the dead by the glory of
the Father, so we also may walk in newness of
life and seek those things which are above, where
with thee, O Father, and the Holy Spirit, he
liveth and reigneth for ever and ever.

### –510– *Easter*

O risen and victorious Christ, whose power and
love destroyed the darkness and death of sin;
Ascend, we pray thee, the throne of our hearts,
and so rule our wills by the might of that immortality wherewith thou hast set us free, that
we may evermore be alive unto God, through
the power of thy glorious resurrection; world
without end.

### –511– *Whitsunday*

O God, who as at this time didst teach the hearts
of thy faithful people, by sending to them the
light of thy Holy Spirit; Grant us by the same

Spirit to have a right judgment in all things, and evermore to rejoice in his holy comfort; through the merits of Christ Jesus our Saviour, who liveth and reigneth with thee, in the unity of the same Spirit, one God, world without end.

*–512– Whitsunday*

O God, who in the exaltation of thy Son Jesus Christ dost sanctify thy universal Church; shed abroad in every race and nation the gift of his Spirit; that the work wrought by his power at the first preaching of the gospel may be extended throughout the whole world; through the same our Lord Jesus Christ, who liveth and reigneth with thee in the unity of the same Spirit now and ever.

*–513– Whitsunday*

O Almighty God, Who on the day of Pentecost didst send the Holy Ghost the Comforter to abide in Thy Church unto the end: bestow upon us and upon all Thy faithful people His manifold gifts of grace, that with minds enlightened by His truth, and hearts purified by His presence, we may day by day be strengthened with power in the inward man; through Jesus Christ our Lord, Who with Thee and the same Spirit liveth and reigneth, one God, world without end.

*–514– Whitsunday*

God, who didst give thy Holy Spirit to guide and strengthen thy faithful people, and to bind them into one fellowship; fill us now with the same Spirit, that our hearts may be on fire to love thee; and loving thee, to love one another; through Jesus Christ our Lord.

*–515– Whitsunday*

O God, who in all ages hast sent thy power to sanctify the faithful: Let the flame of thy Spirit so kindle and cleanse thy Church, that in purity and strength we may present unto thee the glad oblation of our lives; through Jesus Christ our Lord.

*–516– New Year's Eve*

Most gracious God, Who hast been merciful unto us in the year that is past, and hast guided and upheld us through all the years of our life on earth: we beseech Thee to pardon our sins and to make us abound in faith and love; fashion in us those virtues which are acceptable unto Thee, and grant that we may serve Thee more faithfully in the year that is to come; through Jesus Christ our Lord.

*–517– New Year's Day*

Immortal Lord God, who inhabitest eternity, and hast brought us, thine unworthy servants, to the beginning of another year: Pardon, we most humbly beseech thee, our transgressions in the past, and graciously abide with us all the days of our life; guard and direct us in all trials and temptations, that by thy blessing we may grow in grace as we grow in years, and at the last may finish our course with joy; through Jesus Christ our Lord.

*–518– For the New Year*

O God, who art from everlasting to everlasting, and hast vouchsafed to us a new beginning of days; grant us, we pray Thee, throughout this year, such prosperity as Thou seest to be good for us, and make us to abound in such works as are pleasing unto Thee. As days and years pass over us, teach us to be more thankful for past mercies, more penitent for past faults, and more earnest to serve Thee in the years that Thou shalt give us, that so we may look forward with increasing joy to the new year of eternal life; through Jesus Christ our Lord.

# XXIX

## Peace

*–519–* *For International Fellowship*

O God, who hast appointed a day when the kingdoms of this world shall become the Kingdom of our Lord and of his Christ; Quicken our loyalty to thee that we may now and always choose thy will as our will, thy way as our way, thy peace as our peace. So lock our fortunes to thy purpose (in these days of perplexity) that we may be satisfied with nothing less than a world at unity with itself; and, in abiding fellowship, win for mankind that freedom and mutual trust which will enable all nations to bring their glory and honor into thy Kingdom; through him who came to set men free, Jesus our King.

*–520–* *For the Family of Nations*

Almighty God, our heavenly Father, guide, we beseech thee, the Nations of the world into the way of justice and truth, and establish among them that peace which is the fruit of righteousness, that they may become the Kingdom of our Lord and Saviour Jesus Christ.

### –521– *For Peace*

Almighty God, from whom all thoughts of truth
and peace proceed; kindle, we pray thee, in the
hearts of all men the true love of peace; and
guide with thy pure and peaceable wisdom those
who take counsel for the nations of the earth;
that in tranquillity thy Kingdom may go forward, till the earth be filled with the knowledge
of thy love: through Jesus Christ our Lord.

### –522– *For Governments and the Comity of Na-tions*

Almighty God, who alone givest wisdom and understanding; inspire, we pray thee, the minds of
all to whom thou hast committed the responsibility of government and leadership in the nations of the world. Give to them the vision of
truth and justice, that by their counsel all nations and classes may work together in true
brotherhood, and thy Church may serve thee
in unity and peace; through Jesus Christ our
Lord.

### –523– *Foreign Policy*

Teach us, O Lord, to see every question of for-
eign policy in the light of our creed; that we
may check in ourselves and in others every temper which makes for war, all ungenerous judgments, all promptings of self-assurance, all pre-

sumptuous claims; and grant that being ever
ready to recognize the needs and aspirations of
other nations, we may, with patience, do whatsoever in us lies to remove suspicions and mis-
understandings; and to honor all men in Jesus
Christ our Lord.

## –524– *World Peace*

O God, by whose quickening grace we are made
fellow-citizens of the household of faith: Grant
that the good endeavors of thy people in all nations, fitly framed together, may grow unto a
holy temple of righteousness and truth; through
him who is our peace, thy Son, Jesus Christ our
Lord.

## –525– *For the Will to Keep Peace*

O God, who hast put into the hearts of men
a great longing for peace but hast also given to
man the power to choose: Grant us the will to
make our choices in accordance with thy will.
Bind the world together, O God, in fellowship,
service, and love, and grant that we may take
our part in the fulfilment of thy purpose;
through Jesus Christ our Lord.

## –526– *Liberty and Righteousness*

O eternal God, through whose mighty power
our fathers won their liberties of old; Grant,
we beseech thee, that we and all the people of

this land may have grace to maintain these liberties in righteousness and peace; through Jesus Christ our Lord.

### –527– *Humility with Firmness*

O God, who hast given us the grace to carry the sword of thy Kingdom of peace; who hast made us messengers of peace in a world of strife, and messengers of strife in a world of false peace: make strong our hand, make clear our voice, give us humility with firmness and insight with passion that we may fight not to conquer, but to redeem.

### –528– *For the Nations*

O Holy Ghost, who leadest the faithful into all truth: Enable us, we pray thee, so fervently to reveal the Gospel in our lives, that all nations may be brought out of darkness and error into the clear light and true knowledge of Jesus Christ our Lord, whom with thee and the Father we worship and glorify as one God, world without end.

### –529– *For Fellowship Among the Nations*

Almighty God, who art the Father of all men upon the earth, most heartily we pray that thou wilt keep thy children from cruelties of war, and lead the nations in the way of peace. Teach

us to put away all bitterness and misunderstanding, both in church and state; that we, with all the brethren of the Son of Man, may draw together as one comity of peoples, and dwell evermore in the fellowship of that Prince of Peace, who liveth and reigneth with thee in the unity of the Holy Spirit, now and ever.

## –530– *For International Goodwill*

Almighty God, who alone givest wisdom and understanding; inspire with thy Holy Spirit all who bear the responsibility of government in the nations of the world. Give them the vision of truth, that they may set the needs of the common people above the desire for power or the defence of glory, and the nations work together in true brotherhood, through Jesus Christ our Lord.

## –531– *Comradeship*

O God, our Father, give to the nations of the world a new heart of comradeship, that each may bring its tribute of excellence to the common treasury, and all the world go forward in the new and living way which Christ hath consecrated for us; who liveth and reigneth with thee and the Holy Spirit, one God, world without end.

*–532– A Prayer of Nations*

Almighty God, supreme Governor of all men:
Incline thine ear, we beseech thee, to the prayer
of nations, and so overrule the imperfect counsel of men, and set straight the things they cannot govern, that we may walk in the paths of
obedience to places of vision, and to thoughts
that purge and make us wise; through Jesus
Christ our Lord.

*–533– For All Christians*

Look with thy mercy, O Father of men, upon
all thy children in every land, on every sea, and
in the thoroughfares of the sky. Hold in thy
gracious keeping every burdened heart, encourage every noble hope, strengthen every righteous
purpose. Unite in the deathless bond of charity
all followers of thy valiant Son, whose Name,
and whose Name alone, can still the cries of
greed and bring to our stricken world the
hush of peace. Shatter our fears and our misgiv-
ings, and let the light of truth so govern our
thoughts and guide our hands that, with all the
brotherhood of the sons of God, we may receive as our home that kingdom which belongs
to thy Son, our Saviour Jesus Christ.

### –534– *An International Conference*

O God, Who art the lover of justice and peace: direct, we beseech Thee, the minds and wills of those who are called to deliberate for the welfare of the nations and the peace of the world; that as faithful stewards of the things which belong unto righteousness, they may have regard to Thy laws and the true welfare of mankind. And so guide them by Thy Holy Spirit, that by word and deed they may promote Thy glory, and set forward peace and mutual goodwill among men; through Jesus Christ our Lord.

### –535– *In Time of Crisis*

O God, Who hast knit together in one family all the nations of the earth: remove far from us, we beseech Thee, the menace of war: pour out upon the rulers of the peoples Thy spirit of peace; restrain the passions of such as plan aggression; and hasten the time when the kingdoms of this world shall become the kingdom of Thy Son, our Saviour Jesus Christ.

### –536– *Atomic Power*

Almighty and merciful God, without Whom all things hasten to destruction and fall into nothingness: look, we beseech Thee, upon Thy family of nations and men, to which Thou hast com-

mitted power in trust for their mutual health and comfort. Save us and help us, O Lord, lest we abuse Thy gift and make it our misery and ruin; draw all men unto Thee in Thy kingdom of righteousness and truth; uproot our enmities, heal our divisions, cast out our fears; and renew our faith in Thine unchanging purpose of good-will and peace on earth; for the love of Jesus Christ our Lord.

## –537– *For the Space Age*

O God of interstellar space, in whose sight a thousand years are as an evening gone; enlarge our horizons, we beseech thee, that we may behold thy majesty in all thy works and know thy lordship in all thy ways.

## –538– *For the Space Age*

Almighty God, whose creative hand we discern in the vastness of the oceans, the strength of the hills, and the unimaginable reaches of space; Grant that as we enter more deeply into the mysteries of the world which thou hast wrought, we may never forget thy loving purpose for us and for all men, lest we perish in ignorance of the things belonging to our peace; through our Lord and Saviour Jesus Christ.

# XXX

## FAMILY PRAYERS

### –539– *For a Blessing on the Families of the Land*

Almighty God, our heavenly Father, who settest the solitary in families; We commend to thy continual care the homes in which thy people dwell. Put far from them, we beseech thee, every root of bitterness, the desire of vain-glory, and the pride of life. Fill them with faith, virtue, knowledge, temperance, patience, godliness. Knit together in constant affection those who, in holy wedlock, have been made one flesh; turn the heart of the fathers to the children, and the heart of the children to the fathers; and so enkindle fervent charity among us all, that we be ever-more kindly affectioned with brotherly love; through Jesus Christ our Lord.

### –540– *A Home*

Be present with us, O Lord, in our daily duties, and grant to those Who dwell in this house the strength and protection of Thy continual help; that Thou mayest be known as the Master of the family and the defender of this home; through Jesus Christ our Lord.

*-541- Our Households*

O Eternal God, who alone makest men to be of one mind in a house; Help us faithfully to fulfil our duties as members of our several households. Put far from us all unkind thoughts, anger, and evil speaking. Give us tender hearts, full of affection and sympathy toward all. Grant us grace to feel the sorrows and trials of others as our own, and to bear patiently with their imperfections. Preserve us from selfishness, and grant that, day by day, walking in love, we may grow up into the likeness of Thy blessed Son, and be found ready to meet Him, and to enter with Him into that place which He has gone to prepare for us; for His sake, who liveth and reigneth with Thee and the Holy Ghost ever, one God, world without end.

*-542- On a Wedding Anniversary*

Heavenly Father, we give thee heartfelt thanks, on this anniversary of the day when we were made one in holy matrimony, for thy blessing upon us then and for thy continual mercies until now. We thank thee that our love has deepened with the passing days and for all the joys of our home and family life. Renew thy blessing upon us now, we beseech thee, as we renew our vows of love and loyalty, and may thy Holy Spirit strengthen us that we may ever remain

steadfast in our faith and in thy service; through Jesus Christ our Lord.

### -543- *This Family and Household*

Almighty God, who art the author of all goodness, look down in mercy upon this family and household and bless all who belong to it, present or absent. Save and defend us in all dangers and adversities, give us all things that are needful to our souls and bodies, and bring us safely to thy heavenly kingdom; through Jesus Christ our Lord.

### -544- *Bearing One Another's Burdens*

O God, Who art perfect love, grant that we who are born of Thee, and eat of Thy bread, may bear one another's burdens with sincere affection; that Thy peace which passeth all understanding may keep our hearts and minds in Christ Jesus Thy Son our Lord, Who with Thee and the Holy Ghost liveth and reigneth one God, world without end.

### -545- *A Happy Home*

O God, our Father, we thank thee for our home and family; for love and forbearance, for friends and foes, for laughter enjoyed and sorrow shared, for the daily bread of thy bounty in good times and bad. Help us to be mindful of thy gifts and

glad to show forth thy praise; through Jesus
Christ our Lord.

### –546– *Parents' Thanksgiving*

We thank thee, O God our Father, for giving
us this our child to bring up for thee. Help us
as true disciples to set *him* a good example in
all we think or say or do. Keep *him* well in
body and mind; and grant that *he* may grow
in grace and in the knowledge and love of thy
Son, our Saviour, Jesus Christ.

### –547– *A Prayer for Parents*

Deliver us, good Lord, from the excessive demands of business and social life that limit family
relationships; from the insensitivity and harshness of judgment that prevent understanding;
from domineering ways and selfish imposition of
our will; from softness and indulgence mistaken
for love. Bless us with wise and understanding
hearts that we may demand neither too much
nor too little, and grant us such a measure of
love that we may nurture our children to that
fulness of manhood and womanhood which thou
hast purposed for them; through Jesus Christ
our Lord.

### –548– *For Young People*

O Lord Jesus Christ, we pray thee that our
young people who are growing in independence,

may be ready to be guided by thee. May they trust thee who art the truth, and put themselves in thy hands who art the way and the life. Teach them what to aim for, what to believe and what to do, so that their lives may be built on the everlasting verities.

## –549– *Our Family*

Lord, behold our family here assembled. We thank Thee for this place in which we dwell; for the love that unites us; for the peace accorded us this day; for the hope with which we expect the morrow; for the health, the work, the food and the bright skies that make our lives delightful; for our friends in all parts of the earth.

Give us courage, gaiety and the quiet mind. Spare to us our friends, soften to us our enemies. Bless us, if it may be, in all our innocent endeavors. If it may not, give us the strength to encounter that which is to come, that we may be brave in peril, constant in tribulation, temperate in wrath, and in all changes of fortune and down to the gates of death, loyal and loving one to another.

## –550– *On Returning Home*

Lord of our going out and our coming in, I thank Thee for my return home after the day's

round. Whatever the day may have asked or given, Thou knowest how much I have left undone that I should have done, and how much I have done amiss. Accept it all, I pray Thee, as my evening sacrifice. Forgive the faults and failures and, beyond any power of mine, continue and extend whatever has had any promise for Thy cause and Thy kingdom. Save me from vain regrets and from too much anxiety for the morrow. Bless the quiet hours with those I love, and as I commit them and myself to Thee may we all find renewal of spirit in rest and trustful sleep. In Jesus' name.

### –551– *For Friendship*

O God who hast made pleasant and lovely the bonds of friendship, I thank Thee for the many friends and comrades with whom Thou hast enriched my life. Tighten the cords of love which unite us in Thee, and in death divide us not; through Jesus Christ our Lord.

### –552– *For Those Without Family*

O God, who settest the solitary in families, we pray for all who are without children or kin. Relate them in life with those who need their strength and love, and make them one in the fellowship of the Spirit, in the Church of thy dear Son.

# XXXI

## PERSONAL PRAYERS

### –553– *Light of Thy Presence*

Most merciful Father, giver of every good gift, who hast called us to stand in thy house and keep watch over thy people; Forgive us, we beseech thee, all our sins, and remove every trace of them, that they may not darken our minds and make us blind leaders of the blind. Sanctify us with thy truth, kindle our hearts with the love of thy Name, and grant us to walk in the light of thy presence; that ever seeking thee alone we may attain unto thee, and taught of thee may by word and example lead others to thee, the true Shepherd of our souls.

### –554– *For Consecration*

O God, who alone canst uphold the minds of men, without whose beauty and goodness our souls are unfed, without whose truthfulness our reasons wither; Consecrate our lives to thy will, giving us such purity of heart, such depth of faith, such steadfastness of purpose, that, in thy good time, we may come to think thine own thoughts after thee; through Jesus Christ our Saviour.

## -555- *For Strength and Protection*

O God, who knowest us to be set in the midst
of so many and great dangers, that by reason
of the frailty of our nature we cannot always
stand upright; Grant to us such strength and
protection, as may support us in all dangers,
and carry us through all temptations; through
Jesus Christ our Lord.

## -556- *In Our Infirmities*

Lord Jesus, merciful Saviour, who art touched
with the feeling of our infirmities, and hast been
at all points tempted even as we are, yet without sin: we have done amiss and dealt wickedly,
we have sinned against Thee in thought, word,
and deed. Look with compassion upon our weakness, cleanse us from our sins, forgive us both
what we have done and left undone; and give
us grace to amend our lives, to Thy glory Who
hast called us out of darkness into Thy light and
love; we ask it for Thy sake and in Thy Name.

## -557- *For Mercy*

O Thou, who searchest the hearts of men: Look
with mercy upon our sins, especially our sins
against the truth; forgive them and help us to
walk this day in the light. Deliver us from timid
silence; give us courage to speak the truth with

boldness, and grace to speak the truth with love; and save us in thought, word, and deed from the perils of self-deception; through Jesus Christ our Lord.

### –558– *For God's Help*

Blessed Lord, who wast tempted in all things like as we are, have mercy upon our frailty. Out of weakness give us strength. Support us in time of temptation. Embolden us in the time of danger. Help us to do thy work with good courage; and to continue thy faithful soldiers and servants unto our life's end; for thy name's sake.

### –559– *In Time of Temptation*

O God, if thou dost permit us to be taken up into the mount of temptation to see the kingdoms of the world and the glory of them, grant that we may see also the world's need and the fields white already to harvest, that so, by thy grace, we may desire only thy glory and the redemption of our fellowmen, and lose our wills in thine, whose service is perfect freedom; through Jesus Christ our Lord.

### –560– *For Truthfulness*

Almighty God who hast sent the Spirit of truth unto us to guide us into all truth: so rule our lives by thy power that we may be truthful in

thought and word and deed. May no fear or hope ever make us false in act or speech; cast out from us whatsoever loveth or maketh a lie, and bring us all into the perfect freedom of thy truth; through Jesus Christ our Lord.

## –561– *For the Love of God*

O God, whose love is our life, open our hearts, we beseech thee, to receive thy gifts; take away from us coldness and calculation, the blindness of pride and the luxury of hurt feelings; pour out upon us thy quickening Spirit, that our dry places may be green again, and our whole being rejoice in thee; through Jesus Christ our Lord.

## –562– *The Tyranny of Words*

My good Lord Jesus, deliver me from the tyranny of words, that I may hear thee in silence and serve thee with simplicity.

## –563– *For True Religion*

Lord of all power and might, who art the author and giver of all good things; Graft in our hearts the love of thy Name, increase in us true religion, nourish us with all goodness, and of thy great mercy keep us in the same; through Jesus Christ our Lord.

### –564– *Use of Time*

Eternal God, who by the life of thy dear Son hast shown us that there is no minute of our own but we may be doing thy will: Help us to use our time aright, that however we are engaged, in work or leisure or play, we may stand before thee with a pure conscience, acting, speaking and thinking as in thy presence; through the same Jesus Christ our Lord.

### –565– *In God's Sight*

O Heavenly Father, in whom we live and move and have our being, we humbly pray thee so to guide and govern us by thy Holy Spirit, that in all the cares and occupations of our daily life we may never forget thee, but remember that we are ever walking in thy sight; through Jesus Christ our Lord.

### –566– *Prayer When Unable to Sleep*

I am not going to attempt to pray for long now, Lord, or it will keep me awake even more. All I want to say is that I accept this sleeplessness, and unite it to what You suffered on the night of Thursday in Holy Week. I am at least resting and more or less comfortable. You were allowed no moment of rest, no shred of comfort. Often I have deliberately stayed awake at night

for reasons of pleasure, and not particularly com-
plained afterwards: tonight I can make my involuntary wakefulness an act of love. In which
case I must certainly not complain afterwards.
And now, if it is Your will, let me sleep. But if
it is not, it does not matter.

## –567– *For a Sense of Joy*

Grant to us, O Lord, the royalty of inward happiness, and the serenity which comes from living close to thee: Daily renew in us the sense
of joy, and let the eternal spirit of the Father
dwell in our souls and bodies, filling us with
light and grace, so that, bearing about with us
the infection of a good courage, we may be dif-
fusers of life, and may meet all ills and cross
accidents with gallant and high-hearted happiness, giving thee thanks always for all things.

## –568– *For Patience*

When many are coming and going and there is
little leisure, give us grace, O heavenly Father,
to follow the example of our Lord Jesus Christ,
who knew neither impatience of spirit nor confusion of work, but in the midst of all his labours held communion with thee, and even upon
earth was still in heaven; where now he reigneth
with thee and the Holy Spirit world without
end.

### –569– *For Humility*

O God, who through thy Son Jesus Christ hast promised a blessing to the meek upon earth, take from us all pride and vanity, boasting and forwardness; and give us the true courage that shows itself by gentleness, the true wisdom that shows itself by simplicity, and the true power that shows itself by modesty; for Christ's sake.

### –570– *For Our Needs*

Almighty God, the fountain of all wisdom, who knowest our necessities before we ask, and our ignorance in asking; We beseech thee to have compassion upon our infirmities; and those things which for our unworthiness we dare not, and for our blindness we cannot ask, vouchsafe to give us, for the worthiness of thy Son Jesus Christ our Lord.

### –571– *For One Whose Ministry Seems Ineffective*

Almighty God, I thank thee for the vision of service that brought me to thy ministry, and for thy many blessings in the past. Give me patience, I beseech thee, in my dry season; help me to see good will in my people, strengthen my weakness, increase my faith, sustain me in the communion of saints, and restore in me a measure

of usefulness in the good companionship of Jesus Christ our Lord.

### —572— *In Failure*

O God, whose blessed Son was despised and rejected of men, help us to accept our failures as real and necessary instructions in our pilgrimage toward freedom and wholeness in Jesus Christ our Saviour.

### —573— *For Daily Self-Surrender*

O God, in obedience to thy command, I surrender myself to thee this day, all that I am and all that I have, to be unconditionally thine for thy using. Take me from myself and use me as thou wilt, where thou wilt, when thou wilt, with whom thou wilt; for Christ's sake.

### —574— *In Weakness, Strength*

O God, who hast made us so strong and so weak, in our weakness hold us to Thee, in our strength let us hold to Thee, through Jesus Christ our Lord.

### —575— *For the Presence of God*

Lord, be thou within me, to strengthen me; without me, to keep me; above me, to protect me; beneath me, to uphold me; before me, to direct

me; behind me, to keep me from straying; round about me, to defend me. Blessed be thou, our Father for ever and ever.

## –576– *The Heavenly Vision*

Grant unto us, O Lord, the heavenly vision; that we may behold not only the things of sense in their turmoil and transience, but the things that remain in their rest and everlastingness. Grant us the sweet graces of the eternal years, and may we ever rejoice in the duties that bring with them a quiet heart; through Jesus Christ our Lord.

## –577– *For All for Whom We Ought to Pray*

We call to mind, O God, before Thy throne of grace, all those whom Thou hast given to be near and dear to us, and all for whom we are especially bound to pray, beseeching Thee to remember them all for good, and to fulfil, as may be expedient for them, all their desires and wants. We commend to Thee any who may have wronged us, whether by word or deed, beseeching Thee to forgive them and us all our sins, and to bring us to Thy heavenly kingdom, through Jesus Christ our Lord.

### -578- *For True Joys*

O Almighty God, who alone canst order the unruly wills and affections of sinful men; Grant unto thy people, that they may love the thing which thou commandest, and desire that which thou dost promise; that so, among the sundry and manifold changes of the world, our hearts may surely there be fixed, where true joys are to be found; through Jesus Christ our Lord.

### -579- *Commendation*

We commend unto thee, O Lord,
   our souls and our bodies,
   our minds and our thoughts,
   our prayers and our hopes,
   our health and our work,
   our life and our death;
   our parents and brothers and sisters,
   our benefactors and friends,
   our neighbours, our countrymen,
and all Christian folk
   this day and always.

### -580- *Tranquility*

   Lord, temper with tranquility
     our manifold activity,
   That we may do our work for thee
     with very great simplicity.

# XXXII

## MEDITATION

O Lord my God, I am not worthy that thou
shouldest come under my roof; yet thou hast
honoured thy servant with appointing him to
stand in thy House, and to serve at thy holy
Altar. To thee and to thy service I devote myself, body, soul, and spirit, with all their powers
and faculties. Fill my memory with the words
of thy Law; enlighten my understanding with
the illumination of the Holy Ghost; and may
all the wishes and desires of my will center in
what thou hast commanded. And, to make me
instrumental in promoting the salvation of the
people now committed to my charge, grant that
I may faithfully administer thy holy Sacraments,
and by my life and doctrine set forth thy true
and lively Word. Be ever with me in the performance of all the duties of my ministry: in
prayer, to quicken my devotion; in praises, to
heighten my love and gratitude; and in preaching, to give a readiness of thought and expres-
sion suitable to the clearness and excellency of
thy holy Word. Grant this for the sake of Jesus
Christ thy Son our Saviour.

### *–582– For the Coming of the Holy Spirit*

Blessed Spirit of God, come to us in all thy fullness and power, to enrich us in our poverty, to inflame us in our feebleness. Be closer to us than breathing, nearer than hands or feet. As the branches are in the vine, so may we abide in thee. Compass our minds with thy wisdom. Saturate our souls with thy righteousness. Fire our wills with thy might. Melt our hearts with thy love. Do everything at all times to make us wholly thine until thy wealth is ours and we are lost in thee; through Jesus Christ our Lord.

### *–583– For Guidance*

O Lord Jesus Christ, who art the Way, the Truth, and the Life; We pray thee suffer us not to stray from thee, who art the Way, nor to distrust thee, who art the Truth, nor to rest in any other thing than thee, who art the Life. Teach us, by thy Holy Spirit, what to believe, what to do, and wherein to take our rest.

### *–584– The Love of Christ*

O God our Father, grant unto us according to the riches of thy glory to be strengthened with might by thy spirit in the inner man, that Christ may dwell in our hearts by faith; that we, being rooted and grounded in love, may be able

to comprehend with all saints what is the breadth, and length, and depth, and height of thy glorious purpose, and know the love of Christ which passeth knowledge, that we may be filled with the fullness of God.

## –585– *The Everlasting Truth*

Lift up, we beseech thee, O Christ, our hearts and our spirits above the false show of things, above fear and melancholy, above laziness and despair, above selfishness and covetousness, above custom and fashion, up to the everlasting truth and order that thou art; that so we may live joyfully and freely, in the faith and trust that thou art our King and our Saviour, our example and our judge, and that as long as we are loyal to thee all will be well with us in this world, and in all worlds to come.

## –586– *Our Calling*

O God, the Holy Spirit, who hast called us to be prophets, and who showest to them that love thee the things that were and the things that are and the things that shall be hereafter; before we dare to speak of thee to others, reveal thyself to us. Breathe into our hearts the mysteries which no man can learn except by prayer. Take every faculty which thou hast given and make it servant to every trust which thou dost reveal. Give us thy message, save us from our own; then help

us to utter, without fear and without favor, each word of thine. Thou hast called us also to be thy priests, to live in heaven, yet on earth, to talk with thee and to speak with men; Make us, we beseech thee, deeply sensible of the sacredness of our calling. Turn our thoughts from titles and robes to love and sacrifice. When we stand at thine altar, when we walk in the highway, when we counsel men in darkness, when we go among the sick, the dying, and the dead, grant us always so plainly to see thy heaven, that we may show it upon earth. All which we ask through Jesus Christ our Lord.

## —587— *Daily Prayer of Personal Dedication*

Almighty God our heavenly Father, I thank Thee that Thou art the sovereign Lord of my spirit, my mind, and my body, and that "the law of the Spirit of life in Christ Jesus hath made me free from the law of sin and death." O Lord and Lover of my soul, I thank Thee that Thou art ever breathing into me the power and love of Thy Holy Spirit, so that from my soul there may ever shine forth the light, the love, the joy, the power, and the peace of Thy presence. I thank Thee that moment by moment Thou art cleansing, strengthening, sustaining, healing, and guiding me. All that I now so freely receive from Thee, dear heavenly Father, help me freely to give again, that my life this day may be a channel of Thy divine life, for the

coming of Thy Kingdom, for the cleansing of
all sin, and for the healing of all sickness throughout the world; through Jesus Christ our Lord.

## –588– *My Daily Prayer*

Lord, make me an instrument of thy peace,
Where there is hatred, let me sow love;
Where there is injury, pardon;
Where there is doubt, faith;
Where there is despair, hope;
Where there is darkness, light; and
Where there is sadness, joy.
O, Divine Master, grant that I may not so much
    seek to be consoled as to console;
To be understood as to understand;
To be loved as to love,
For it is in giving that we receive;
It is in pardoning that we are pardoned.
And it is in dying that we are born to eternal
    life.

## –589– *The Fight of Faith*

Almighty and everlasting God, by whose grace
thy servants are enabled to fight the good fight
of faith, and ever to prove victorious, I humbly
beseech thee to strengthen me by thy mighty
power for the battle of life; that in thy strength
I may fight my sins and temptations and overcome them.

Inspire me with thy Holy Spirit that I may think wisely, speak rightly, resolve bravely, act kindly, live purely. Bless me in body and soul and make me a blessing to others. May my chief aim always be to do my duty faithfully to thee, and to my fellow men. Let the assurance of thy Presence strengthen me in life and comfort me in death, O Lord my God, for Jesus Christ's sake.

## –590– *Kindle My Heart*

O true light, which lightenest every man that cometh into this world, lighten my eyes that I sleep not in death.

O fire that ever burnest and never failest, I am lukewarm, yes, cold: kindle my heart that it may be on fire with love of thee.

O King of heaven and earth, rich in mercy, I am poor and needy; then help me, O my God, and out of the treasury of thy goodness enrich my soul.

## –591– *On Using Time*

O Eternal God, who hast created me to do the work of God after the manner of men, and to serve Thee in this generation, and according to my capacities; give me Thy grace that I may

be a prudent spender of my time, so as I may best prevent or resist all temptation, and be profitable to the Christian commonwealth; and, by discharging all my duty, may glorify Thy name. Take from me all slothfulness, and give me a diligent and an active spirit, and wisdom to choose my employment; that I may do works proportionable to my person, and to the dignity of a Christian, and may fill up all the spaces of my time with actions of religion and charity; improving my talent entrusted to me by Thee, my Lord, that I may enter into the joy of the Lord, to partake of Thy eternal felicities, even for Thy mercy's sake.

## –592– Returning to God

I ask, dear Lord, that Thou wouldst make me wholly Thine. Penetrate me wholly with Thyself, that Thou mayest be all in all in me; be Thou the Soul of my soul. Lord, I am weary of myself, weary of being so unlike Thee, of being so far away from Thee. Abide with me, then,—abide in me. Let no sorrow keep me away from Thee; let no loneliness or desolation of soul affright me. Let me not think of Thee as one afar off; let me not think of Thee as a severe judge, since Thou Thyself comest unto me, and fallest on the neck of Thy poor prodigal, and givest me the kiss of peace. Thou wilt not let those go empty away who come to Thee from far. Lord, I am come to Thee from far, the

far-off land of my miseries and my sins. But
Thou hast brought me nigh.

## -593- *The Cloud of Witnesses*

Our heavenly Father, we rejoice in the blessed
communion of all Thy saints, wherein Thou
givest us also to have part. We remember before Thee all who have departed this life in Thy
faith and love, and especially those most dear to
us. We thank Thee for our present fellowship
with them, for our common hope, and for the
promise of future joy. O, let the cloud of wit-
nesses, the innumerable company of those who
have gone before, and entered into rest, be to
us an example of godly life, and even now may
we be refreshed with their joy; that so with
patience we may run the race that yet remains
before us, looking unto Jesus, the author and
finisher of our faith; and obtain an entrance into
the everlasting kingdom, and glorious assembly
of the saints, and with them ever worship and
adore Thy glorious Name, world without end.

## -594- *The House of the Soul*

O God, the Light of every heart that sees Thee,
the Life of every soul that loves Thee, the
Strength of every mind that seeks Thee, grant
me ever to continue steadfast in Thy holy love.
Be Thou the joy of my heart; take it all to Thyself, and therein abide. The house of my soul

is, I confess, too narrow for Thee; do Thou enlarge it, that Thou mayest enter in: it is ruinous, but do Thou repair it. It has that within which must offend Thine eyes; I confess and know it; but whose help shall I implore in cleansing it but Thine alone? To Thee, therefore, I cry urgently, begging that Thou wilt cleanse me from my secret faults, and keep Thy servant from presumptuous sins, that they may never get dominion over me.

## -595- *Body and Spirit*

O eternal God, sanctify my body and soul, my thoughts and my intentions, my words and actions, that whatsoever I shall think, or speak, or do, may be by me designed for the glorification of Thy Name, and, by Thy blessing, it may be effective and successful in the work of God, according as it can be capable. Lord, turn my necessities into virtue, the works of nature into the works of grace, by making them orderly, regular, temperate; and let no pride or self-seeking, no covetousness or revenge, no little ends and low imaginations, pollute my spirit, and unhallow any of my words and actions; but let my body be a servant of my spirit, and both body and spirit servants of Jesus; that, doing all things for Thy glory here, I may be partaker of Thy glory hereafter, through Jesus Christ our Lord.

## -596- *Words and Deeds*

I offer up unto Thee my prayers and intercessions, for those especially who have in any matter hurt, grieved, or found fault with me, or who have done me any damage or displeasure.

For all those also whom, at any time, I may have vexed, troubled, burdened, and scandalized, by words or deeds, knowingly or in ignorance; that Thou wouldst grant us all equally pardon for our sins, and for our offences against each other. Take away from our hearts, O Lord, all suspiciousness, indignation, wrath, and contention, and whatsoever may hurt charity, and lessen brotherly love.

Have mercy, O Lord, have mercy on those that crave Thy mercy, give grace unto them that stand in need thereof, and make us such as that we may be worthy to enjoy Thy grace, and go forward to life eternal.

## -597- *God's Forbearance*

O Lord my God, for life and reason, nurture, preservation, guidance, education; for Thy gifts of grace and nature, for Thy calling, recalling, manifold recalling me again and again; for Thy forbearance, long-suffering, and long long-suf-

fering toward me, even until now; for all from whom I have received any good or help; for the use of Thy present good things; for Thy promise, and my hope, of good things to come; for all these things, and for all other, which I know not, manifest or secret, remembered or forgotten by me, I praise Thee, I bless Thee, I give Thee thanks, all the days of my life. What shall I render unto the Lord for all His benefits to me? Thou art worthy, O Lord, to receive glory, and honour, and power.

## –598– *Arrow Prayers*

O God, set our hearts at liberty from the service of ourselves, and let it be our meat and drink to do thy will; through Jesus Christ our Lord.

## –599–

Almighty God, give me the power to rejoice over other men's brightness and strength and success; through him who laid down his life for his friends, our Master Jesus Christ.

## –600–

O Lord of life, make our lives clear spaces where children may find happiness and law; through Jesus Christ our Lord.

-601-

Bless us, O God, with the vision of Thy being and beauty, that in the strength of it we may do our work without haste and without rest.

-602-

Lord, help us to remember what we ought not to forget, and to forget what we ought not to remember.

-603-

Teach us to pray often; that we may pray oftener.

-604-

Lord, that which we have prayed against in the morning, suffer us not to have done before the evening.

-605-

O Lord, never suffer us to think that we can stand by ourselves, and not need thee.

-606-

Lord, make thy will our will in all things.

–607–

Lord, give us grace to do what we can, that thou mayest empower us to do what thou wilt.

–608–

O Lord, forgive what I have been, sanctify what I am; and order what I shall be.

–609–

Make us to remember, O God, that every day is Thy gift, to be used according to Thy command.

–610–

O Thou who knowest me so utterly, help me to know thee a little.

–611–

Lord, I am not yet willing for thee to have thy way with me, but I am willing to be made willing.

–612–

Teach us, O Lord, to fear Thee without being afraid; to fear Thee in love that we may love Thee without fear.

*–613–*

Teach me, O my Lord Jesus, instruct me, that I may learn from Thee what I ought to teach concerning Thee.

*–614–*

O Lord, baptize our hearts into a sense of the conditions and needs of all men.

*–615–*

O God, make us children of quietness, and heirs of peace.

*–616–*

O God, help us not to despise what we do not understand.

*–617–*

Thou that hast giv'n so much to me,
Give one thing more, a grateful heart.

*–618–*

Those things, good Lord, that we pray for, give us thy grace to labor for.

*–619–*

O God, grant us patience to plant the seed and be content, nor doubt thy faithfulness to bring the harvest.

*–620–*

Teach us to care and not to care.

*–621–*

O God, help us to be masters of ourselves that we may be servants of others.

*–622–*

Keep us, Lord, so awake in the duties of our callings that we may sleep in thy peace and wake in thy glory.

# XXXIII

## Prayers for a Retreat

### –623– *At the Beginning*

O Almighty God, Whose blessed Son held communion with Thee in the retirement of solitary places, look mercifully, we beseech Thee, upon Thy servants who, following His example, do seek in solitude and silence, refreshment for our souls and strength for Thy service, and grant that we may be abundantly blessed; through the Same, Thy Son, Jesus Christ our Lord.

### –624– *Before the Addresses*

O Lord God Almighty, without Whose aid no man can either deliver or receive Thy word; grant us, we beseech Thee, the help of Thy Holy Spirit, that at this time Thy message may be both faithfully proclaimed and joyfully accepted, to Thy glory, the benefit of Thy Church, and the welfare of our souls; through Jesus Christ our Lord.

### –625– *Before the Addresses*

Assist us, O Lord, we pray Thee, in our thinking and praying, that our minds may be enlight-

ened to know Thy will for us, and our wills set upon obedience to the same; through Jesus Christ our Lord.

### –626– *Before the Addresses*

Grant us, O Lord, we pray Thee, the help of Thy Holy Spirit, that our minds may know Thee, our hearts may love Thee, that our lips may praise Thee that our lives may glorify Thee; through Jesus Christ our Lord.

### –627– *At the End*

Look mercifully, we pray Thee, O Lord, upon us Thy servants as we go away again into our own homes, and grant that we, being risen with Thee, may ever seek those things which are above, where Thou, together with the Father and the Holy Ghost, dost live and reign, One God, blessed for evermore.

### –628– *For a Retreat or Quiet Day*

O Lord Jesus Christ, who didst say to thine Apostles "Come ye apart into a desert place and rest awhile," for there were many coming and going; grant, we beseech thee, to thy servants here gathered together, that they may rest awhile at this present time with thee. May they so seek thee, whom their souls desire to love, that they may both find thee and be found of thee. And

grant such love and such wisdom to accompany
the words which shall be spoken in thy name,
that they may not fall to the ground, but may
be helpful in leading us onward through the
toils of our pilgrimage to that rest which re-
maineth to the people of God; where, neverthe-
less, they rest not day and night from thy perfect service; who with the Father and the Holy
Ghost livest and reignest ever one God, world
without end.

### –629– *Help Thou Our Unbelief*

Lord God, we believe in thee, help thou our
unbelief; we love thee, yet not with a perfect
heart as we would; we long to serve thee, yet
not with our full strength; we trust in thee, yet
not with our whole mind. Forgive our past dis-
loyalties, accept our present purposes, and grant
us thy blessing, through Jesus Christ our Lord.

### –630– *Amendment of Life*

Grant, I beseech Thee, merciful Lord that the
designs of a new and better life, which by Thy
grace I have now formed, may not pass away
without effect. Incite and enable me, by Thy
Holy Spirit, to improve the time which Thou
shalt grant me; to avoid all evil thoughts, words,
and actions; and to do all the duties which Thou
shalt set before me. Hear my prayer, O Lord,
for the sake of Jesus Christ.

### –631– *For Pardon*

Pardon, O God, our offences, done voluntarily or involuntarily, wittingly or unwittingly, by word or deed or in thought; forgive those that are hidden and those that are manifest, those which were done long ago, those which are known, and those which are forgotten, but are known unto Thee. Forgive us, O God, through Jesus Christ our Lord.

### –632– *For Control of Speech*

Almighty God, who knowest how often we sin against thee with our lips; Consecrate our speech to thy service, and keep us often silent, that our hearts may speak to thee and listen for thy voice; through Jesus Christ our Lord.

### –633– *For Restraint in Criticism*

O Lord, Jesus Christ, who didst show unfailing patience and generosity in thy judgment of the people round thee; Forgive us the careless criticism and unkind words which cause so much suffering to others; help us neither to coin cruel gossip nor give currency to it, but rather to seek the best that lies in everyone and use it to the glory of thy Name.

## –634– *For a Forgiving Spirit*

Deliver us, O God, from injustice, envy, hatred, and malice; give us grace to pardon all who have offended us, and to bear with one another even as thou, Lord, dost bear with us, in thy patience and great loving-kindness; through Jesus Christ our Lord.

## –635– *Christ in Us*

Lord, who hast warned us that without thee we can do nothing; and by thy holy Apostle hast taught us that in thy strength we can do all things: So take and possess us, that our weakness may be transformed by thy power; that we be no longer our own, but thine; that it be not we who live, but thou who livest in us; who now reignest with the Father and Holy Spirit, world without end.

## –636– *Strength against Sin*

O Thou who wast strong enough to bear all our sins: Impart to us thy strength that we may sin no more; for thy tender mercy's sake.

## –637– *Self-Knowledge*

O God, who art never deceived: Dispel the blindness of our heart; and so quicken our con-

science that we may see ourselves as thou all-truly seest us; for Jesus Christ's sake.

Forgive us, merciful God, the sins which have so laid hold upon us that we no longer confess them to be sins. Let thy Spirit enlighten us, thy love cleanse us, thy grace strengthen us; through Jesus Christ our Lord.

### —638— *For Right Choice*

O Lord the only wise, the God and Father of all, who hast shown unto man light and darkness, right and wrong, that he may choose freely between them: Grant us both generosity and courage to choose the good and to refuse the evil, that we may be numbered among thy sons in whom thou art well-pleased, and who dwell in thy presence; through Jesus Christ our Lord.

### —639— *The Everlasting Love*

O good Jesus, who alone orderest my life and my days; worthless and unworthy, I cast myself upon thine infinite love. I trust thee with my all: with my present and my future; with my joys and my sorrows; with my time and my eternity. Deal with me as thou willest and knowest best, only bind me fast with the bonds of thine everlasting love.

## -640- *God's Purpose in My Life*

Lord, undertake for me. Quiet my selfish clamoring. Be Thou my sufficiency. All things happen according to Thy ordering. And if Thou orderest my life, there can be no room for anything but joy when Thy decree goeth forth; for Thy ordering is alone secure. No planning or scheming of mine will mar Thy plan for me. Nothing remains for me but to fit myself into Thy plan. And so shall I reach my highest good and find opportunity for my highest, fullest service. Lord, be Thou my peace. Lay hold on my faculties and train them to Thy use. Inspire me with undying devotion to Thee and Thy will. I am afraid of my weakness. Let it be a vessel to hold Thy strength. Let me not break, O God. Fill me with Divine power, through Jesus Christ our Lord.

## -641-

O Lamb of God, that takest away the sins of the world, have mercy upon us.

O Lamb of God, that takest away the sins of the world, have mercy upon us.

O Lamb of God, that takest away the sins of the world, grant us thy peace.

# NOTES

1. William Reed Huntington (d. 1909), *Materia Ritualis* (1882). The Book of Common Prayer (abbreviated BCP) 1928.
2. John Austin (seventeenth century).
3. Edmund Gibson (d. 1748), Bishop of London (1723-48), *Family Devotion: or a Plain Exhortation to Morning and Evening Prayer in Families* (1705). BCP 1789.
4. Charles Henry Brent (d. 1929), Bishop of the Philippine Islands (1901-18), Western New York (1918-29), *With God in Prayer* (1907).
5. Greek Church Liturgy (third century).
6. Mozarabic Liturgy (*c.* 600).
7. Rowland Williams (d. 1870), *Psalms and Litanies, Counsels and Collects, for Devout Persons* (1872). BCP 1928.
8. Bishop Brent, *With God in Prayer* (1907).
9. Benjamin Jenks (d. 1724).
10. William Bright (d. 1901), Canon of Christ Church, Oxford (1868-1901), *Ancient Collects* (1861). BCP 1928.
11. Bishop Brent, *With God in Prayer* (1907).
12. *Prayers New and Old*, ed. by Clement W. Welsh.
13. In a number of medieval books this appears as an end paper.
14. Traditional.
15. Bishop Brent, *With God in Prayer* (1907).
16. George Edward Lynch Cotton (d. 1866), Bishop of Calcutta (1858-66). BCP 1892, revised 1928.
17. *Prayers for the Church Service League* (1952 ed.), The Protestant Episcopal Diocese of Mass., p. 87.
18. *A Book of Prayers for Students* (1920). The Student Christian Movement Press.

*19.* BCP 1549.

*20.* *The Gothic Missal* (seventh century), translated by William Bright. BCP 1928.

*21.* *Gelasian Sacramentary* (494). BCP 1549.

*22.* Bishop Stephen Fielding Bayne, Jr. (b. 1908), *Prayers for the Diocese of Olympia.*

*23.* *Leonine Sacramentary* (440).

*24.* Bishop Brent, *With God in Prayer* (1907).

*25.* William Reed Huntington, *Materia Ritualis* (1882). BCP 1928.

*26.* The Office of Compline.

*27.* Bishop Brent, *With God in Prayer* (1907).

*28.* From the conclusion of sermon, "Wisdom and Innocence," preached by John Henry Newman in 1834 (probably from a sixteenth-century source). BCP 1928.

*29.* Fifteenth-century English, found in Sarum Primers.

*30.* Collects of the Ordinal (1550). BCP 1662.

*31.* The Scottish Prayer Book.

*32.* Henry Sylvester Nash (d. 1912), *A Selection of the Prayers of Henry Sylvester Nash,* ed. by J. W. Suter.

*33.* The Church Army (U. S. A.)

*34.* After Jeremy Taylor (d. 1667), Bishop of Down, Connor, and Dromore (1662-67). From *Prayers for Our Ministry* (1916), arranged by Thomas Frederick Davies, Bishop of Western Massachusetts (1911-36).

*35.* *The Priest's Prayer Book* (1897), ed. by Littledale and Vaux.

*36.* After William Laud (d. 1645), Archbishop of Canterbury (1633-45). From *Prayers for Our Ministry* (1916).

*37.* *Prayers for Today* (1918), compiled by Samuel McComb.

*38.* The Editor.

*39.* Sherman Elbridge Johnson (b. 1908), Dean of The Church Divinity School of the Pacific. Adapted from the Ordinal, BCP 1928, p. 539.

40. Dean Johnson.
41. An ancient collect, BCP.
42. *The Kingdom, the Power and the Glory,* the American Edition of the Grey Book (1933), No. 59.
43. *Prayers for the Minister's Day* (1946), The Pilgrim Press.
44. Dr. Samuel Johnson (d. 1786).
45. Unknown.
46. From a collect in *The Manual of Intercessory Prayer,* published by Richard Meux Benson, S.S.J.E. (d. 1915). BCP 1928.
47. The Editor.
48. The Editor.
49. Francis J. Moore (b. 1885), *Prayers for All Occasions.*
50. The Editor.
51. Henry Sylvester Nash, *A Selection of the Prayers of Henry Sylvester Nash,* ed. by John W. Suter.
52. Francis J. Moore, *Prayers for All Occasions.*
53. *Prayers for the Church Service League,* The Protestant Episcopal Diocese of Mass., p. 54.
54. *The Book of Offices* (1940), The Church Pension Fund.
55. The Editor.
56. Richard Feller (b. 1919).
57. Francis J. Moore, *Prayers for All Occasions.*
58. *A Book of Prayers* (1957), ed. by John Heuss, p. 40.
59. The Editor.
60. The Editor.
61. *A Book of Prayers* (1957), ed. by John Heuss, p. 66.
62. The Editor.
63. The Editor.
64. Francis J. Moore, *Prayers for All Occasions.*
65. The Editor.
66. Francis J. Moore, *Prayers for All Occasions.*
67. *A Book of Prayers,* adapted from BCP 1928, p. 43.
68. Francis J. Moore, *Prayers for All Occasions.*

69. The Editor.
70. John Wallace Suter (b. 1890), *Prayers of the Spirit* (1943).
71. After Percy Dearmer, Canon of Westminster (d. 1936), *The Prayer Manual* (1951), ed. by Canon Macnutt.
72. *The Kingdom, the Power and the Glory* (1933), No. 35.
73. Francis J. Moore, *Prayers for All Occasions*.
74. G. C. Binyon, *Prayers for the City of God* (1920).
75. Francis J. Moore, *Prayers for All Occasions*.
76. *Prayers New and Old*, ed. by Clement W. Welsh.
77. George Lyman Locke (d. 1919). BCP 1928.
78. John Wallace Suter, *Prayers of the Spirit*.
79. *Book of Prayers* (1954), ed. by Leon and Elfrieda McCauley, p. 50.
80. Francis J. Moore, *Prayers for All Occasions*.
81. Robert J. Plumb (b. 1900).
82. Robert J. Plumb.
83. *The Kingdom, the Power and the Glory*, No. 67.
84. *A Book of Prayers for Students*, The Student Christian Movement Press.
85. Dean Johnson.
86. Dean Johnson.
87. The Editor.
88. The Editor.
89. The Editor.
90. The Editor.
91. Ashton Oxenden, Bishop of Montreal (d. 1892).
92. *The Kingdom, the Power and the Glory*, No. 78.
93. The Canadian Prayer Book.
94. Douglas H. Crick, Bishop of Chester, from *The Prayer Manual*, ed. by Canon Macnutt, p. 210.
95. Carol Christopher Drake (b. 1933).
96. The Editor.
97. William Boyd Carpenter (d. 1918), Bishop of Ripon, from *A Chain of Prayer Across the Ages*, ed. by Selina F. Fox, p. 262.
98. The Editor.

99. *Let Us Pray* (1959), The General Assembly of the Church of Scotland, p. 23.
100. Max. R. Drake (b. 1920).
101. Derwent A. Suthers (b. 1931).
102. The Editor.
103. Francis J. Moore, *Prayers for All Occasions*.
104. *The Book of Offices* (1949), The Church Pension Fund.
105. Francis J. Moore, *Prayers for All Occasions*.
106. Herman Page (d. 1939), Bishop of Michigan (1923-39).
107. Unknown.
108. Dr. Samuel Johnson.
109. *The Kingdom, the Power and the Glory*, No. 81.
110. The Editor.
111. The Editor.
112. A. L. Illingworth (d. 1878), from *A Chain of Prayer Across the Ages*, ed. by Selina F. Fox, p. 261.
113. BCP 1928.
114. The Editor.
115. *A Book of Prayers*, ed. by John Heuss, p. 40.
116. The Editor.
117. The Editor.
118. *Parent's Prayers* (1953), compiled by Muriel Streitbert Curtis.
119. St. Paul's Cathedral, London, from *Prayers in Ministry*, ed. by Canon Macnutt, p. 202.
120. Leslie S. Hunter, Bishop of Sheffield, *New Every Morning* (1936).
121. BCP 1928.
122. John Wallace Suter, *Prayers of the Spirit*.
123. John Wallace Suter, *A Book of Collects* (1919). BCP 1928.
124. *Prayers for the Church Service League*, The Protestant Episcopal Diocese of Mass., p. 76.
125. After St. Paul (Eph. 3:14-19).
126. The Editor.
127. The Editor.
128. The Scottish Prayer Book, 1912. BCP 1928.

129. After Thomas à Kempis (1379-1471).
130. *Prayers New and Old*, ed. by Clement W. Welsh.
131. *A Book of Prayers for Students* (adapted), The Student Christian Movement Press.
132. *Let Us Pray*, The General Assembly of the Church of Scotland, p. 79.
133. Francis J. Moore, *Prayers for All Occasions*.
134. BCP 1549.
135. Preface to the Geneva Bible (1560).
136. *Prayers New and Old*, ed. by Clement W. Welsh.
137. The Editor and Dean Johnson.
138. The Scottish Prayer Book.
139. Dean Johnson.
140. Henry Sylvester Nash, *A Selection of the Prayers of Henry Sylvester Nash*, ed. by John W. Suter.
141. Dean Johnson.
142. Henry Sylvester Nash, *A Selection of the Prayers of Henry Sylvester Nash*, ed. by John W. Suter.
143. Christina Rossetti (d. 1894).
144. Dr. Samuel Johnson.
145. Dr. Samuel Johnson.
146. Dr. Samuel Johnson.
147. George Ridding, Bishop of Southwell (d. 1904).
148. *The London Service Book* (1948), ed. by George W. Briggs, Canon of Worcester, p. 59.
149. *The Priest's Prayer Book*, ed. by Littledale and Vaux.
150. *Prayers for the Minister's Day*, The Pilgrim Press.
151. *Prayers for Our Ministry*, ed. by Thomas F. Davies.
152. *Prayers for the Minister's Day*, The Pilgrim Press.
153. The Editor.
154. The Editor.
155. *The Book of Offices* (1949), The Church Pension Fund.
156. Bishop Brent, *With God in Prayer* (1907).
157. An ancient collect.
158. Derwent A. Suthers.
159. *The Book of Offices* (1949), The Church Pension Fund.

*160.* Ibid. p. 63.

*161.* BCP 1928.

*162.* *The Book of Offices* (1949), The Church Pension Fund.

*163.* Ibid. p. 50.

*164.* Frederick B. Macnutt, Canon of Canterbury (d. 1950), *The Prayer Manual* (1952).

*165.* Francis J. Moore, *Prayers for All Occasions.*

*166.* *Gregorian Sacramentary* (591). BCP 1549.

*167.* Richard Meux Benson, *Manual of Intercessory Prayer.*

*168.* *Prayers New and Old,* ed. by Clement W. Welsh.

*169.* Blessings from several sources, mainly biblical.

*170.* *Prayers for the Church Service League,* The Protestant Episcopal Diocese of Mass., p. 109.

*171.* Miles Lowell Yates (d. 1956), *Our Bounden Duty,* p. 110.

*172.* Ibid. p. 110.

*173.* Unknown.

*174.* Charles Lewis Slattery (d. 1930), Bishop of Massachusetts (1927-30), *Prayers for Private and Family Use* (1922).

*175.* The Editor.

*176.* The Prayer Book of the Church of Ireland.

*177.* The Editor.

*178.* Miles Lowell Yates, *Our Bounden Duty,* p. 111.

*179.* Hugh L. Johnston, *The Prayer Manual,* compiled by F. B. Macnutt.

*180.* The Scottish Prayer Book.

*181.* John Wallace Suter, *Prayers of the Spirit.*

*182.* Richard Meux Benson, *Manual of Intercessory Prayer.* BCP 1928.

*183.* Miles Lowell Yates, *Our Bounden Duty,* p. 109.

*184.* Ibid.

*185.* *When Two or Three* (1932).

*186.* Unknown. Adapted by J. W. Suter.

*187.* A. S. T. Fisher, ed., *An Anthology of Prayers.*

*188.* George Dawson (d. 1870).

*189.* John Wallace Suter, *Prayers of the Spirit.*

*190.* Ibid.

*191.* Ibid.

*192.* Ibid.

*193.* William Reed Huntington. BCP 1928.

*194.* John Wallace Suter, *A Book of Collects.* BCP 1928.

*195.* BCP 1552.

*196.* Thomas Wilson (d. 1775), Bishop of Sodor and Man.

*197.* The Editor.

*198.* The Editor.

*199.* Arthur C. A. Hall (d. 1930), Bishop of Vermont (1894-1930), *Prayers for Our Ministry,* compiled by Bishop Davies.

*200.* John Charles Vaughan (d. 1897), Dean of Llandaff (1879-87).

*201.* Miles Lowell Yates, *Our Bounden Duty.*

*202.* Traditional.

*203.* Traditional.

*204.* *Gelasian Sacramentary.* BCP 1549.

*205.* Edward White Benson (d. 1896), Archbishop of Canterbury (1883-96).

*206.* Bishop Brent, *With God in Prayer* (1907).

*207.* Unknown.

*208.* John Lydney (sixteenth century).

*209.* Unknown.

*210.* Archbishop Laud.

*211.* Traditional, Western.

*212.* Traditional, Western.

*213.* Traditional, Eastern Orthodox.

*214.* BCP 1549.

*215.* BCP 1552.

*216.* Sarum Office of Compline. BCP 1928.

*217.* *Lutheran Manual of Prayer.*

*218.* St. Augustine (d. 430), Bishop of Hippo.

*219.* Willard L. Sperry (d. 1954), Dean of the Harvard Divinity School, *Prayers for Private Devotions in War-time.*

*220.* Reinhold Niebuhr (b. 1892).

*221.* John Donne (d. 1631).

222. *When Two or Three.*
223. Unknown.
224. Unknown. BCP 1928.
225. Unknown.
226. James Martineau (d. 1900).
227. *Mozarabic Liturgy,* translated by William Bright.
228. *Coptic Liturgy of St. Cyril* (fifth century), translated by William Bright.
229. Bishop Jeremy Taylor.
230. Bishop Brent, *With God in Prayer* (1907).
231. *Hope and Courage* (1944).
232. Richard Meux Benson, *An Anthology of Prayers,* ed. by A. S. T. Fisher.
233. *Gregorian.* BCP 1549.
234. John Wallace Suter, *Prayers of the Spirit.*
235. *Leonine* and *Gelasian.* BCP 1549.
236. John Wallace Suter, *Prayers of the Spirit.*
237. Unknown. BCP 1928.
238. Miles Lowell Yates, *Our Bounden Duty.*
239. St. Augustine.
240. The Canadian Prayer Book.
241. The South African Prayer Book.
242. The Editor.
243. The Editor.
244. *Hope and Courage* (1944).
245. BCP 1928.
246. John Wallace Suter, *Prayers of the Spirit.*
247. Church of Ireland Prayer Book.
248. The Editor.
249. The Canadian Prayer Book.
250. BCP 1928.
251. Church of Ireland Prayer Book.
252. The Editor.
253. Unknown.
254. Bishop Brent, *With God in Prayer* (1907).
255. *Collects and Prayers; for Use in Church.*
256. *Army and Navy Service Book.*
257. Henry Sylvester Nash, *A Selection of the Prayers of Henry Sylvester Nash,* ed. by John W. Suter.

*258.* Diana Ponsonby.

*259.* *Daily Prayer,* ed. by Eric Milner-White and George W. Briggs, p. 34.

*260.* Arthur H. Wright, *Prayers for Priest and People,* ed. by John Wright, The Church Book Co., St. Paul, 1899.

*261.* The Editor.

*262.* The Editor.

*263.* *Sarum,* condensed in William Bright's *Ancient Collects,* altered slightly for BCP 1928.

*264.* John Cosin (d. 1672), Bishop of Durham. BCP 1928.

*265.* The Editor.

*266.* Bishop Charles Lewis Slattery, *Prayers for Private and Family Use* (1922). BCP 1928.

*267.* Church of Ireland Prayer Book.

*268.* *Hope and Courage* (1944).

*269.* BCP 1549.

*270.* Unknown.

*271.* The Scottish Prayer Book.

*272.* The South African Prayer Book.

*273.* Arranged by Armen D. Jorjorian (b. 1919).

*274.* Unknown.

*275.* BCP 1928.

*276.* John Wallace Suter, *Prayers of the Spirit.*

*277.* Ibid.

*278.* Ibid.

*279.* Church of Ireland Prayer Book.

*280.* Charles Morris Addison (d. 1947). BCP 1928.

*281.* Francis J. Moore, *Prayers for All Occasions.*

*282.* Ibid.

*283.* *Hope and Courage* (1944).

*284.* Ibid.

*285.* Bishop Brent, *With God in Prayer* (1907).

*286.* Unknown.

*287.* John Wallace Suter, *Prayers of the Spirit* (abbreviated).

*288.* *Prayers of Health and Healing,* Student Christian Movement Press, p. 70.

*289.* Church of Ireland Prayer Book.

290. The Editor.
291. *Sarum.* BCP 1928.
292. Unknown. BCP 1928.
293. BCP 1928.
294. Charles Lewis Slattery, *Prayers for Private and Family Use* (1922). BCP 1928.
295. *Burial Services* (1958), compiled by Joseph B. Bernardin.
296. *The Occasional Services,* The United Lutheran Church in America, p. 136.
297. John Dowden (d. 1910), Bishop of Edinburgh. BCP 1928.
298. *Hope and Courage* (1944).
299. The Scottish Prayer Book.
300. The Editor.
301. The Editor.
302. Canon R. W. D. Lee, *The Prayer Manual,* compiled by F. B. Macnutt.
303. *Burial Services,* compiled by Joseph B. Bernardin, p. 50.
304. *Hope and Courage* (1944).
305. *The Priest's Prayer Book* (1890). BCP 1892.
306. Bishop Slattery, *Prayers for Private and Family Use* (1922). BCP 1928.
307. William Bright. BCP 1928.
308. BCP 1928.
309. *The Kingdom, the Power and the Glory,* p. 61.
310. Church of Ireland Prayer Book.
311. Church of South Africa Prayer Book.
312. *Burial Services* (1958), compiled by Joseph B. Bernardin, p. 68.
313. Church of Ireland Prayer Book.
314. John Wallace Suter, *Prayers of the Spirit.*
315. Bishop Brent, *With God in Prayer* (1907).
316. *The Kingdom, the Power and the Glory,* No. 75.
317. Ibid. No. 76.
318. The Editor.
319. Charles F. Whiston (b. 1900).

*320.* Bishop Slattery, *Prayers for Private and Family Use* (1922).

*321.* *Prayers for the Minister's Day*, The Pilgrim Press.

*322.* *Prayers New and Old*, ed. by Clement W. Welsh.

*323.* William Bright, *Ancient Collects*. BCP 1928.

*324.* *The Kingdom, the Power and the Glory*, No. 41.

*325.* The Daily Service: *Prayers and Hymns for Schools* (1947), ed. by G. W. Briggs.

*326.* Edward Lambe Parsons (b. 1868), retired Bishop of California.

*327.* G. C. Binyon, *Prayers for the City of God*.

*328.* William Bright, *Ancient Collects*. BCP 1928.

*329.* Christina Rossetti.

*330.* Unknown.

*331.* *Prayers New and Old*, ed. by Clement W. Welsh.

*332.* Miles Lowell Yates, *Our Bounden Duty*, p. 75.

*333.* Unknown.

*334.* Bishop Edward Lambe Parsons.

*335.* William Bright, *Ancient Collects.* BCP 1928 (slightly altered).

*336.* Fifth century. BCP 1552.

*337.* BCP 1549.

*338.* After Bishop Arthur C. A. Hall. From *Prayers for Our Ministry*.

*339.* Max L. Drake.

*340.* The Editor.

*341.* Charles F. Hall (b. 1908), Bishop of New Hampshire.

*342.* Max L. Drake.

*343.* The Editor.

*344.* Dean Johnson.

*345.* Henry Sylvester Nash, *A Selection of the Prayers of Henry Sylvester Nash*, ed. by John W. Suter.

*346.* Gelasian. BCP 1549 (altered 1662).

*347.* *A Devotional Diary*, J. H. Oldham.

*348.* Unknown.

*349.* Unknown.

*350.* The Editor.

*351.* Traditional.

*352.* Unknown.

*353.* St. Richard of Chichester (d. 1253).

*354.* After St. Augustine.

*355.* John Wallace Suter, *Prayers of the Spirit.*

*356.* The Scottish Prayer Book.

*357.* *The Kingdom, the Power and the Glory* (1933), p. 73.

*358.* An ancient collect.

*359.* Rabanus Maurus (d. 856), translated by Bishop Cosin. BCP 1662.

*360.* BCP.

*361.* Miles Lowell Yates, *Our Bounden Duty,* p. 26.

*362.* Ibid. pp. 21-2.

*363.* Based on BCP 1928, p. 83.

*364.* An ancient collect. BCP 1549.

*365.* St. Thomas Aquinas (d. 1274). Newly translated (1959) by Massey Hamilton Shepherd, Jr. O God, who under a wonderful Sacrament hast left unto us the memorial of thy Passion: Grant us, we beseech thee, so to reverence the sacred Mysteries of thy Body and Blood, that we may always perceive within ourselves the fruit of thy redeeming work; who livest and reignest with the Father, in the unity of the Holy Ghost ever, one God, world without end.

*366.* John Wallace Suter, Sr. (d. 1942). BCP 1928.

*367.* John Wallace Suter, *Prayers of the Spirit.*

*368.* *Leonine.*

*369.* Miles Lowell Yates, *Our Bounden Duty,* p. 83.

*370.* *Prayers for the Church Service League* (1952), Protestant Episcopal Diocese of Mass.

*371.* Basically *Gelasian.* BCP 1892.

*372.* Unknown.

*373.* Unknown.

*374.* Unknown.

*375.* *A Book of Prayers,* ed. by John Heuss, p. 92.

*376.* BCP 1928.

*377.* Unknown.

*378.* Canon Macnutt, *The Prayer Manual.*

*379.* William Fisher Lewis (b. 1902), Bishop of Olympia.

*380.* Francis J. Moore, *Prayers for All Occasions.*

*381.* Canon Macnutt, *The Prayer Manual.*

*382.* *Prayers for the Church Service League,* The Protestant Episcopal Diocese of Mass.

*383.* *Gelasian.*

*384.* Church of Ireland Prayer Book.

*385.* Unknown.

*386.* Archbishop Laud, *A Summarie of Devotions* (1667). BCP 1928.

*387.* BCP 1549.

*388.* BCP 1928.

*389.* *Gelasian.* BCP 1549.

*390.* Francis J. Moore, *Prayers for All Occasions.*

*391.* The Editor.

*392.* *The London Service Book,* ed. by George W. Briggs, p. 64.

*393.* Ibid.

*394.* William Reed Huntington, *Book of Offices and Prayers* (1886). BCP 1928.

*395.* *Gregorian.* BCP 1549.

*396.* BCP 1549 (altered 1928).

*397.* The Scottish Prayer Book.

*398.* *Prayers for the Church Service League,* The Protestant Episcopal Diocese of Mass.

*399.* *Prayers New and Old,* ed. by Clement W. Welsh.

*400.* Ibid.

*401.* Francis J. Moore, *Prayers for All Occasions.*

*402.* Unknown.

*403.* *Prayers New and Old,* ed. by Clement W. Welsh.

*404.* Ibid.

*405.* Manual of St. Augustine's College, Canterbury.

*406.* Bishop Thomas Wilson.

*407.* *Daily Prayer,* ed. by Eric Milner-White and George W. Briggs, pp. 99-100.

*408.* Eric Milner-White (b. 1884), Dean of York, *After the Third Collect.*

*409.* Frederick Dan Huntington (d. 1904), Bishop of Central New York. BCP 1928.

*410.* BCP 1928.

*411.* BCP 1928.

*412.* William Reed Huntington, *Materia Ritualis.* BCP 1928.

*413.* *The Kingdom, the Power and the Glory* (1933), No. 69.

*414.* Ibid. No. 70.

*415.* Unknown.

*416.* The Canadian Prayer Book.

*417.* Dean Johnson.

*418.* Dean Johnson.

*419.* Dean Johnson.

*420.* Henry Sylvester Nash, *A Selection of the Prayers of Henry Sylvester Nash,* ed. by John W. Suter.

*421.* The Industrial Christian Fellowship, *The Prayer Manual,* ed. by Canon Macnutt.

*422.* Reinhold Niebuhr.

*423.* After Walter Rauschenbusch. *Prayers of the Social Awakening* (1910).

*424.* *The Boy's Prayer Book.*

*425.* George Appleton, *In His Name.*

*426.* *The London Service Book* (1948), ed. by Canon George W. Briggs, p. 68.

*427.* Unknown.

*428.* The Order of the Knights of the Garter (fourteenth century).

*429.* Thomas Cranmer (d. 1556), Archbishop of Canterbury (1553-56).

*430.* William Temple (d. 1944), Archbishop of Canterbury, *The Abiding Presence.*

*431.* Dean Eric Milner-White.

*432.* *When Two or Three.*

*433.* Helen Beck.

*434.* Miles Lowell Yates, *Our Bounden Duty,* p. 107.

*435.* Ibid.

*436.* Ibid. p. 108.

*437.* Ibid.

*438.* Bishop Brent.

*439.* Francis J. Moore, *Prayers for All Occasions.*

440. *Prayers New and Old,* ed. by Clement W. Welsh.
441. Charles Palmerston Anderson (d. 1930), Bishop of Chicago (1905-30).
442. *Prayers New and Old,* ed. by Clement W. Welsh.
443. John Wallace Suter, *Prayers of the Spirit.*
444. Unknown. BCP 1892.
445. *Prayers New and Old,* ed. by Clement W. Welsh.
446. John Wallace Suter, *Prayers of the Spirit.*
447. Percy Dearmer (d. 1936), from *The Prayer Manual,* ed. by Canon Macnutt.
448. Prayers of 1585.
449. Eric Fenn, *New Every Morning* (1955).
450. Edward Reynolds (d. 1676), Bishop of Norwich (1661-76). BCP 1662.
451. *Prayers for the Church Service League,* The Protestant Episcopal Diocese of Mass.
452. William A. Knight (d. 1916).
453. After John Donne.
454. Fielding Ould, from *A Chain of Prayer Across the Ages,* ed. by Selina F. Fox, p. 128.
455. Based on BCP 1928, pp. 280, 74.
456. A. S. T. Fisher, *An Anthology of Prayers.*
457. BCP 1789, shortened 1892.
458. Francis J. Moore, *Prayers for All Occasions.*
459. Unknown.
460. Canon Macnutt, based on BCP 1928, p. 265.
461. Unknown.
462. *The Kingdom, the Power and the Glory* (1933), p. 75.
463. *Prayers New and Old,* ed. by Clement W. Welsh.
464. Ibid.
465. John Wallace Suter, *A Book of Collects.* BCP 1928.
466. Unknown.
467. St. Augustine.
468. Greek Church Liturgy (third century).
469. Adapted by E. A. L. Clarke, from *A Chain of Prayer Across the Ages,* ed. by Selina F. Fox, p. 290.
470. Unknown.
471. BCP 1549.

472. *The Prayer Manual* (1952), Canon Macnutt.
473. St. Ambrose (d. 397).
474. *Gelasian.* BCP 1549.
475. John Wallace Suter, *Prayers of the Spirit.*
476. Ibid.
477. John Wallace Suter, Sr.
478. John Wallace Suter, *Prayers of the Spirit.*
479. *Prayers New and Old*, ed. by Clement W. Welsh.
480. *Prayers Ancient and Modern*, ed. by Mary Wilder Tileston, rev. ed. 1937, p. 306.
481. The Scottish Prayer Book.
482. BCP 1549.
483. William A. Knight, from *A Chain of Prayer Across the Ages*, ed. by Selina F. Fox, p. 220.
484. Unknown.
485. Unknown.
486. Unknown.
487. Unknown.
488. *Let Us Pray*, The General Assembly of the Church of Scotland, p. 31.
489. Robert Nelson (d. 1665).
490. *Gregorian.*
491. William Reed Huntington. BCP 1928.
492. Unknown.
493. *Gelasian.*
494. BCP 1549.
495. Cardinal Newman.
496. Bishop Thomas Wilson.
497. *Gelasian.* BCP 1928.
498. Handley C. G. Moule (d. 1920), Bishop of Durham, from *A Chain of Prayer Across the Ages*, ed. by Selina F. Fox, p. 225.
499. *Gregorian.* BCP 1549.
500. BCP 1928.
501. The Office of the Royal Maundy, printed in *The Prayer Manual*, ed. by Canon Macnutt, No. 401.
502. Unknown.
503. *Let Us Pray*, The General Assembly of the Church of Scotland, p. 70.

504. *A Treasury of Devotion* (1869).
505. Unknown.
506. Bishop Brent, *With God in Prayer* (1907).
507. *Gregorian.* BCP 1549.
508. Bishop William Boyd Carpenter, from *A Chain of Prayer Across the Ages*, ed. by Selina F. Fox, p. 233.
509. *The Kingdom, the Power and the Glory* (1933), p. 75.
510. John Wallace Suter, *Prayers of the Spirit.*
511. *Gregorian.* BCP 1549.
512. *The Kingdom, the Power and the Glory* (1933), p. 75.
513. Bishop John Dowden, Bishop of Edinburgh (d. 1910), The Scottish Prayer Book.
514. *The London Service Book,* ed. by George W. Briggs.
515. John Wallace Suter, *Prayers of the Spirit.*
516. Unknown.
517. The Canadian Prayer Book.
518. *Prayers for the Christian Year,* The Committee on Public Worship and Aids to Devotion of the General Assembly of the Church of Scotland.
519. Bishop Brent.
520. Bishop Parsons. BCP 1928.
521. Francis Paget (d. 1911), Bishop of Oxford.
522. *The Kingdom, the Power and the Glory,* p. 83.
523. Ibid. p. 84.
524. John Wallace Suter, *Prayers of the Spirit.*
525. *Book of Prayers,* ed. by Leon and Elfrieda Mc-Cauley, p. 107.
526. Bishop Parsons. BCP 1928.
527. Gregory Vlastos, from *The Church Review,* vol. xv, No. 4, May 1956.
528. John Wallace Suter, *Prayers of the Spirit.*
529. *Prayers New and Old,* ed. by Clement W. Welsh.
530. A. S. T. Fisher, *An Anthology of Prayers.*
531. Percy Dearmer, from *An Anthology of Prayers,* ed. by A. S. T. Fisher.
532. John Wallace Suter, *Prayers of the Spirit.*

533. John Wallace Suter, *Prayers of the Spirit* (one word changed with the permission of the author).
534. Unknown.
535. Unknown.
536. Canon Macnutt, *The Prayer Manual*.
537. The Editor.
538. John W. Suter.
539. Bishop F. D. Huntington (1883). BCP 1928 (slightly altered).
540. *Gelasian* (adapted).
541. Unknown.
542. *Book of Prayers*, ed. by Leon and Elfrieda Mc-Cauley, p. 40.
543. Ibid. p. 36.
544. Edward Bouverie Pusey (d. 1882), Canon of Christ Church, Oxford.
545. The Editor.
546. *Prayers New and Old*, ed. by Clement W. Welsh.
547. Charles S. Martin (b. 1906).
548. *Parent's Prayers* (1953) (shortened), Muriel Streitburt Curtis.
549. Robert Louis Stevenson (d. 1894).
550. *Prayers for the Minister's Day*, The Pilgrim Press.
551. Bishop Brent, *With God in Prayer* (1907).
552. *Book of Prayers*, ed. by Leon and Elfrieda Mc-Cauley, p. 37.
553. Henry Sylvester Nash, *A Selection of the Prayers of Henry Sylvester Nash*, ed. by John W. Suter.
554. Ibid.
555. *Gregorian*. BCP 1549 (altered 1662).
556. Unknown.
557. *New Every Morning*, The British Broadcasting Corporation.
558. Brooke Foss Westcott (d. 1901), Bishop of Durham.
559. Dean Johnson.
560. Bishop Westcott.
561. The Editor.
562. The Editor.
563. *Gelasian*. BCP 1549.

*564.* *Daily Prayer,* ed. by Eric Milner-White and George W. Briggs, p. 46.

*565.* The Church of Ireland Prayer Book.

*566.* Dom Hubert van Zeller, *Praying While You Work,* pp. 96-7.

*567.* Lucy Helen Muriel Soulsby (d. 1927), *An Anthology of Prayers,* ed. by A. S. T. Fisher.

*568.* Dean Vaughan.

*569.* Charles Kingsley (d. 1875), adapted by A. S. T. Fisher.

*570.* BCP 1549.

*571.* The Editor.

*572.* The Editor.

*573.* Charles F. Whiston.

*574.* Robert Arthur Miller (b. 1895), *In Weakness Strength.*

*575.* Lancelot Andrewes (d. 1626), Bishop of Winchester.

*576.* Cheltenham College.

*577.* Gavin Hamilton (d. 1612), Bishop of Galloway.

*578.* *Gelasian.* BCP 1549.

*579.* Bishop Lancelot Andrewes.

*580.* Unknown (sixteenth century).

*581.* William Smith (d. 1801). BCP 1804.

*582.* Bishop Brent.

*583.* Desiderius Erasmus (d. 1536).

*584.* St. Paul (Eph. 3:16-19).

*585.* Charles Kingsley (d. 1875).

*586.* Dean Howard Chandler Robbins (d. 1952), adapted by Canon Theodore O. Wedel (b. 1892).

*587.* Unknown.

*588.* St. Francis of Assisi (d. 1226).

*589.* Edward Swett Rousmaniere (d. 1926), Dean of the Cathedral Church of St. Paul, Boston, Mass.

*590.* Edward Bouverie Pusey.

*591.* Bishop Jeremy Taylor.

*592.* Edward Bouverie Pusey.

*593.* *Book of Prayers* (1851).

*594.* St. Augustine.

595. Bishop Jeremy Taylor.
596. St. Thomas à Kempis.
597. Bishop Lancelot Andrewes.
598. Henry Sylvester Nash, *A Selection of the Prayers of Henry Sylvester Nash*, ed. by John W. Suter.
599. Ibid.
600. Ibid.
601. Ibid.
602. Unknown.
603. Bishop Jeremy Taylor.
604. Dean Vaughan.
605. John Donne.
606. Dean Vaughan.
607. *Daily Prayer*, ed. by Eric Milner-White and George W. Briggs.
608. Unknown.
609. Dr. Samuel Johnson.
610. Unknown.
611. F. B. Meyer, *Arrow Prayers*, compiled by Frederick W. Kates.
612. Christina Rossetti.
613. Archbishop Laud.
614. George Fox (d. 1691).
615. Clement of Rome (d. 95).
616. William Penn (d. 1718).
617. George Herbert (d. 1633).
618. Sir Thomas More (d. 1535).
619. *A Book of Small Prayers*.
620. T. S. Eliot (b. 1888).
621. Sir Alec Paterson (d. 1897).
622. John Donne.
623. James Wareham, *The Conducting of Retreats* (1950), p. 54.
624. Ibid.
625. Ibid. p. 55.
626. Ibid.
627. Ibid.
628. Richard Meux Benson, The Society of St. John the Evangelist.

629. Adapted by A. S. T. Fisher, *An Anthology of Prayers*.

630. Dr. Samuel Johnson.

631. Liturgy of the Syrian Jacobites (fifth century).

632. Unknown.

633. A. S. T. Fisher, *An Anthology of Prayers*.

634. Rydal School Hymnal.

635. *Daily Prayer*, ed. by Eric Milner-White and George W. Briggs, p. 31.

636. Ibid.

637. Ibid.

638. Ibid., p. 46.

639. Unknown.

640. Bishop Brent.

641. *Agnus Dei* (seventh century). BCP 1549.

# INDEX OF SUBJECTS

# INDEX OF AUTHORS

THE REFERENCES ARE TO THE NUMBERS OF THE PRAYERS

317

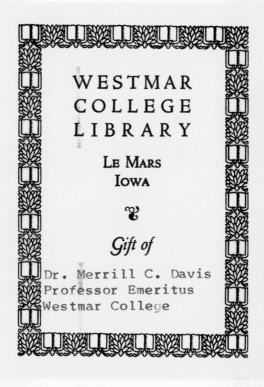

several original prayers written by the editor, and two by Reinhold Niebuhr.

One of the best features of this collection is the extensive and very helpful subject index. There are also several blank pages at the end of this volume where the minister may include some of his favorite personal prayers.

*The Pastor's Prayerbook* will prove an incomparable addition to the Protestant clergyman's library. It holds equal appeal for all denominations, the clergy, seminaries, conventions, conferences, and schools for both its practicality and timeless relevance.

ROBERT N. RODENMAYER is Professor of Pastoral Theology, The Church Divinity School of the Pacific at Berkeley, California. A former chaplain to Episcopal students and faculty at Smith College, he was Chairman of the National College Commission from 1947 to 1952, and Trustee of the General Theological Seminary in 1951-52. Dr. Rodenmayer's books include *Thanks Be To God*, *We Have This Ministry*, and, together with Massey Hamilton Shepherd, Jr., *Our Prayers and Praise*.